Due Return Date Date	Due Return Date Date

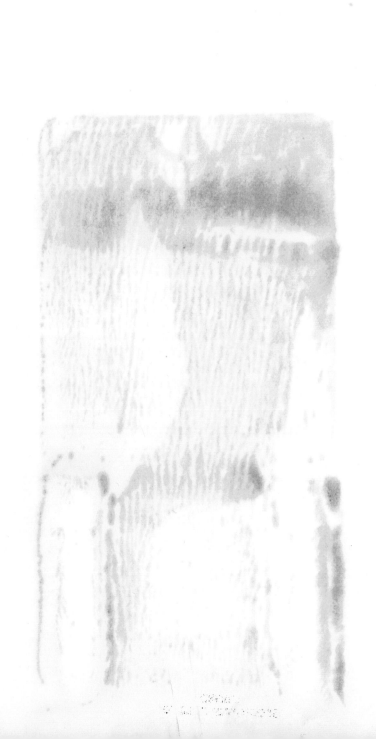

The Dying Gladiators

and other essays

by

Horace Gregory

GREENWOOD PRESS, PUBLISHERS
NEW YORK   1968

Earlier versions of the essays in this collection were previously published in the following books or periodicals, and are reprinted by permission: "Wyndham Lewis: The Artist at War with Himself—1882–1957," *The New York Times Book Review* and *The Commonweal* © 1957 by Commonweal Publishing Co., Inc.; "Poet Without Critics: A Note on Robinson Jeffers," *New World Writing;* "The 'Romantic' Heritage in the Writings of Dylan Thomas," "The Isolation of Isaac Rosenberg," "The Double Vision in Pope's Poetry," and "The Nocturnal Traveller: Walter de la Mare," *Poetry;* "The Gothic Imagination and the Survival of Thomas Lovell Beddoes," *New Republic* and *The Shield of Achilles* © 1944 by Horace Gregory and used by permission of Harcourt Brace & World, Inc.; "Samuel Johnson in the Twentieth Century," *Saturday Review* © 1943 and *The Shield of Achilles* © 1944 by Horace Gregory and used by permission of Harcourt Brace & World, Inc.; "George Moore and Regionalism in Realistic Fiction," *The Shield of Achilles* © 1944 by Horace Gregory and used by permission of Harcourt Brace & World, Inc.; "The Character of F. Scott Fitzgerald," *Herald Tribune Book Review* © 1951 by New York Herald Tribune Inc.; "H. G. Wells: A Wreath for the Liberal Tradition," *New World Writing;* "A Footnote on the Historical Novel," *The New York Times Book Review;* "A Portrait of the Irish as James Joyce," *Evergreen Review* © 1960 by Grove Press, Inc.; "The Dying Gladiators of Samuel Beckett," *The Commonweal* © 1956 by Commonweal Publishing Co., Inc.

Contents

Foreword and a Dedication

My first selection of occasional essays, *The Shield of Achilles* (1944), has long been out of print. Without negating or denying my earlier opinions and convictions, I feel that readers of a generation later would prefer a fresh rearrangement of them, as well as a more mature perspective of the world I hold in view. Therefore the present book contains only three essays chosen from *The Shield of Achilles,* the ones on Samuel Johnson, George Moore, and Thomas Lovell Beddoes; all the others have been written since 1944.

Since 1944 I have often felt that I should do more to clarify my position in respect to the books I read, the writers I thought should be read, and the world I saw behind them. To be fond of reading (as I am) is well enough, but mere bookishness is not. Bookishness is a vice more dangerous than taking daily shots of heroin. It is a vice that afflicts the professional reviewer. With the best of critical intentions, he may hate or love—some or all of them—the books he reviews, yet he becomes almost drugged, almost helpless in the face of what he reads. The serious critic— and I mean serious, not solemn—has to be less professional than that. He must be aware of human motives, the movement of life, behind what he reads. He must also attempt to establish a parity between what he believes is good and the way he voices his conviction. So far, at least, every serious critic is an artist. He cannot afford to allow his writings to drop into the clichés of critical jargon. He is at war against the clichés of his own day.

There are certain duties that the critic owes his readers. One of the most important is to guide them off beaten tracks in reading. It is not in dispraise of Melville or of Henry James that I refuse to offer another essay on them. Nor am I anti-American because I have neglected to write essays on Whitman and Mark Twain. For the past thirty years, they have been "done," redone, and then done again. Today that critical practice is very like selling Frigidaires to the Eskimoes. Doing so might well require great engineering skill and a display of salesmanship—but mere salesmanship is not the concern of any worthy critic.

The individual critic (in his generation at least) should be as singular in his likes and dislikes as the writers who attract his comments. In this respect he should be humane, rather than humanitarian. I happen to be antipolitical. My stress is on the moral, aesthetic, theological implications of what I read. In our day political activities have too often turned against the human spirit. They are nonethical, and incidentally anti-aesthetic.

The present mid-century has seen more than enough of groups and movements—"ideological" groups, political groups, totalitarian states, monolithic states—and under pressures generated by them, the individual as artist, critic, or craftsman, is surrounded by the shadows of authority. But what lies behind some shadows may be transitory. The duty of the critic is to discriminate as best he can among dissenting authorities, to make value judgments, to refresh whatever cultural values have meaning in his age. He should not be intimidated by the past, nor fearful of new ideas. It should be taken for granted that he is well-informed enough not to spread misinformation through ignorance. Since he is human, it should also be taken for granted that he is not free of error.

I hope I have not made my idea of the critic too unearthly to be believed—or too ideal for myself to emulate. As a last touch to his portrait—he should have the courage of his own—not other men's—convictions.

In making a book of the following essays, I am indebted to Barney Rosset for his encouragement. For advice in their selection, I owe many thanks to Marya Zaturenska and Patrick Gregory. In the writing of particular essays, those on Jeffers, H. G. Wells and Samuel Beckett, I am also grateful for the interest shown by Arabel Porter of The New American Library and James Finn of *The Commonweal*.

I dedicate *The Dying Gladiators* to Dr. Theodore Shedlovsky and his wife Beatrice in gratitude for the many years of our continuing friendship; in gratitude for the many evenings we talked, over tea, coffee, or my favorite brand of Irish whiskey, into the hopeful hours of the morning.

Palisades,
Rockland County,
New York
February 15, 1961

The Dying Gladiators

Poet Without Critics:
A Note on
Robinson Jeffers

1

AT THE MOMENT THERE ARE good reasons for rereading the poetry of Robinson Jeffers. First of all, the poet himself is a singular figure in American letters and he occupies the rare position in this country of being a "poet" in the European sense of the word. He insists upon holding to a world view as well as his own handful of currently unpopular opinions. He has become a master of a style without nervous reference to recent fashions in literary criticism. "I can tell lies in prose," he once wrote, which means that his primary concern is with the statement of a few essential poetic truths. Today it is obvious that he is willing to leave a final judgment of what he has written to the decision of posterity.

To reread him is to step aside from the classroom discussions and shoptalk of poetry that flood the rear sections of literary quarterlies where his name is seldom mentioned at all. He is well removed from the kind of company where poetry is "taught" so as to be understood, where critics and reviewers are known to be instructors of literature in colleges and universities. But he is also at some distance from the time when his Californian narratives in verse, "Roan Stallion" and

"Tamar," swept through the furnished rooms and studios of Greenwich Village with the force of an unpredicted hurricane. That was thirty years ago. Today as Jeffers is reread there is no danger of being smothered by the heavily breathing presence of a deep-throated, bare-thighed-and-breasted Jeffers-D. H. Lawrence cult, who had read Freud not wisely but with artless ardor and spent vacations in New Mexico.

Writers like Lawrence and Jeffers who are worshiped by cults, frequently inspire the more violent forms of academic snobbery. Neither came from the "right" prep school, college, or university; neither Oxford or Cambridge could claim Lawrence, nor could the Ivy League universities and colleges in the United States gather their share of glory from Jeffers' reputation. Both Lawrence and Jeffers have outlived their cults; and Lawrence, safely dead and of British origin, no longer irritates the thin, tightly stretched surface of academic temper in the United States. This phenomenon, which is not without its trace of envy, partly explains the neglect, in quarterly reviews, of Jeffers' later writings. It can be said that in recent years Jeffers has been a poet without critics, but this does not mean that his name has been forgotten, his books unread, or his plays in verse neglected on the stage. A few years ago his *Medea* had a respectable run on Broadway, and an off-Broadway theater in New York found audiences for his new play, *The Cretan Woman*.

The initial advantage of rereading Jeffers' poetry now is that it can be approached without the formulas of critical fashions ringing in one's ears. Since 1925 he has published more than fifteen books of verse—a quantity of poetry which resembles the production of his ancestors, the romantic poets of nineteenth-century Britain. Rereading his poems, one finds them falling into three divisions: the Southwestern narratives with their richness of California sea-sky-and-landscape; the shorter poems which are largely conversation pieces—for Jeffers is not a lyric poet—and a fine group of elegies, his

Descent to the Dead, the result of a visit in 1929 to the British Isles; and the semidramatic poems inspired by Greek themes and overlaid with Nietzschean and twentieth-century philosophies.

2

It is best to begin when and where Jeffers' earlier reputation began; the time was 1925 and the place was New York; and credit for the publication of *Roan Stallion, Tamar, and Other Poems* should be given to James Rorty, a writer who met Jeffers during a stay in California and with selfless enthusiasm persuaded New York friends to read "Tamar," to write about it, to make the presence of Jeffers known to New York publishers. Although Jeffers never shared the excitements and diversions of literary circles on the Atlantic Coast, the moment was prepared to receive his semi-Biblical, semi-Sophoclean American Southwestern narratives. Discussions of Steinach operations for restoring sexual vitality were in the air, and so were questions from Krafft-Ebing, Freud, and Jung; D. H. Lawrence's *The Rainbow* was in print as well as Sherwood Anderson's *Dark Laughter.* If a post World War I urban generation had not discovered sex, it had learned to talk loudly and almost endlessly about it. Nothing was easier than to apply cocktail conversations to Jeffers' "Tamar" and "Roan Stallion," which at first reading—and particularly to those who lived in cities—held the same attractions as an invitation to a nudist colony on the Pacific Coast.

Yet it was not without self-critical discernment that Jeffers gave first place to "Tamar" when he prepared his *Selected Poetry* in 1937. For whatever reasons his public had accepted it twelve years earlier, at a time when he had passed the age of thirty-five, the poem has all the merits of a style that he had made his own. As early as 1912 he had paid for the printing of a first book, *Flagons and Apples;* in 1916 a second book, *Californians,* had been published by Macmillan; and neither, aside from the praise of a small group of friends, had received encouragement. His friendships, which included the long-sustained devotion of his wife, Una Call, also embraced the good will of George Sterling, who had known Ambrose Bierce, Joaquin Miller, and Jack London, and who was one of the few to see promise in Jeffers' early books of poems. Like Jeffers, who had been born in Pittsburgh in 1887, Sterling, a native of New York State, had become a converted Californian. Sterling's own verse had been inspired by the pages of *The Savoy* and *The Yellow Book* as well as by readings in Oscar Wilde and Ernest Dowson. "Poetry . . . ," he said, "must . . . cherish all the past embodiments of visionary beauty, such as the beings of classical mythology." Sterling's last work, shortly before his suicide in 1926, was a pamphlet written in praise of Jeffers. No doubt Jeffers had been made aware of the presence of evil through his wide readings, but it was through the loyal patronage of Sterling that he became an heir of "Bitter" Bierce. To the general reader, however, Jeffers' first two books offered little more than glimpses of a belated debt to Dante Gabriel Rossetti in *Flagons and Apples,* and a Wordsworthian manner, which included hints of pantheism, in *Californians.*

Before Jeffers met his wife and Sterling, he had had an unusual education. He was the precocious son of a teacher of theology at Western Theological Seminary in Pittsburgh. His father taught him Greek, Latin, and Hebrew; and when the boy was five and six, took him on trips to Europe. For three years, between the ages of twelve and fifteen, his father sent him to boarding schools in Switzerland and Germany; and at fifteen, Jeffers entered the University of Western Pennsylvania. The next four years were spent in Occidental College and the Universities of Zurich and Southern California, and these years included studies in medicine and forestry. All this would be of no importance if it did not throw light on the individual ranges of Jeffers' poetry, his familiarity with Greek and Roman and Biblical themes, with German philosophy, with medical terms and semiscientific details, and—since he read French with facility—his possible knowledge of the writings of Sade. Certainly his education[1] provided reasons for an affinity with Sterling, whose idea of poetry embraces, however vaguely, "beings of classical mythology." At the very least, Jeffers is a writer whose early years had prepared him for more than a regional view of the world and its affairs.

A second reading of "Tamar" reveals it as a Biblical story in Californian undress. Characters in Jeffers' Southwestern narratives, from "Tamar" to "The Loving Shepherdess," from "Give Your Heart to the Hawks" to "Hungerfield," are often lightly clothed and are subject to the wind, sun, and rain of Californian climate. Chapter 13 of the second book of Samuel is one source of Jeffers' parable,[2] which contains the story of Amnon's love for his sister Tamar. Other associations taken from the two books of Samuel permeate the poem, for the sons of Samuel "walked not in his ways, but turned aside after lucre and took bribes, and perverted judgment," a statement which is appropriate to Jeffers' view of America and Western civilization. As a parable the poem acquires the force of a Calvinist sermon from an American pulpit, yet it also carries within it echoes of Nietzsche's speech of Silenus, "What is best of all is beyond your reach forever: not to be born, not to *be*, to be

---

[1] Jeffers' education was of a kind familiar to well-to-do European gentry of the nineteeth century, but considerably less so to young Americans of the same period. Exceptions in the United States were Henry James's early travels with his father, and the continued educations after college of Longfellow, Trumbull Stickney, George Cabot Lodge, and Henry Adams. Jeffers' development as a narrative poet also follows the precedent of many major nineteenth-century poets; Jeffers and his writings are "in the tradition."

[2] For biographical information concerning Jeffers, as well as the fact that one of the sources of "Tamar" may be found in the second book of Samuel, I am indebted to Lawrence Clark Powell's *Robinson Jeffers: The Man and His Work*.

nothing," and behind these words Sophocles' remark, "Not to be born is best for man." In Tamar's words the echoes are clearly heard: "O God, I wish / I too had been born too soon and died with the eyes unopened. . . ." Jeffers also puts into the mouth of Tamar a remark which has its origins in the doctrines of Sade "we must keep sin pure / Or it will poison us, the grain of goodness in a sin is poison. / Old man, you have no conception / Of the freedom of purity." And as Tamar speaks she has given herself over to unchecked forces of evil. In Sade's novel *Justine,* his heroine is tortured because she fails to purge her taint of goodness; as the poem nears its end, the whipping of Tamar by her brother is the last love scene between them.

This is not to say that Jeffers by voicing echoes of Sade's doctrines had advanced them as examples for Californians to follow; it is rather that he has given the forces of evil a well-established voice of authority, but in doing so he has succeeded with such vehemence that he might be misunderstood by a careless reader. Even at this risk, he has also succeeded in giving the unleashed forces of hell refreshed reality. In his poem, the house of David, Tamar's father—and Tamar is the daughter of King David in the second book of Samuel—is destroyed by fire which in its first association creates a literal image of hell and, in its second, of the funeral pyres of the Romans.

So far I have mentioned only the principal elements of "Tamar," its Californian setting, one of the sources of its story, and a few of the concepts which are made relevant to the re-telling of the story—but these do not complete the list of associations that the poem brings to mind, for "Tamar," beneath the surface of a swiftly moving plot, has a richness of detail which rivals the complex fabric of Elizabethan dramatic verse. In the Biblical story the seduction of Tamar by Amnon is scarcely more than an invitation to come to bed; in Jeffers'

version the seduction scene has an Ovidian ring; a hidden
stream, a pool tempts brother and sister; naked, they enter it
and one recalls Ovid's stories of Narcissus and Echo, Her-
maphroditus and Salmacis, and by association there is a particularly Roman touch, a glimpse of Phoebus' chariot wheel,
from a window of David's house overlooking the Pacific:

> It was twilight in the
> room, the shiny side of the wheel
> Dipping toward Asia; and the year dipping toward
> winter encrimsoned the grave spokes of sundown. . . .

It is this kind of richness that places "Tamar" among the
major accomplishments in twentieth-century poetry. And
what of the ghosts that haunt the house of David in "Tamar"?
They are very like the images of guilt that invade the darkened
walls of Macbeth's castle. An idiot sets fire to David's house,
and one thinks of the line ". . . a tale told by an idiot, full of
sound and fury." In this instance, an idiot hastens the end of
sound and fury.[3]

How deliberate Jeffers was in making a highly individual
combination of Californian locale, Biblical and Græco-Roman

---

[3] In Jeffers' short poem "Self-Criticism in February," there are the following lines which describe the nature of his ghosts, his romanticism, his
unchurched belief in God:

It is certain you have loved the beauty of storm, disproportionately.
But the present time is not pastoral, but founded
Of violence, pointed for more massive violence: perhaps it is not
Perversity but need that perceives the storm-beauty.
Well, bite on this: your poems are too full of ghosts and demons,
And people like phantoms—how often life's are—

. . . .

> *you have never mistaken*
> *Demon nor passion nor idealism for the real God.*
> Then what is most disliked in those verses
> Remains most true.

themes, Elizabethan richness of detail, plus Nietzschean ethics and Calvinist denouements, it is impossible to say. The great probability is that, having a deeply felt desire to warn the world of the dangers of its involvements in world wars, Jeffers brought all the resources, conscious or hidden, of his imagination into play. To Jeffers, World War I was a warning of weaknesses inherent in a civilization that permitted mass murders and a situation that approached total war. War, by example, creates a precedent for violent action; and in "Tamar" that conclusion is shown by the desire of Tamar's brother to leave his father's house to go to war, not merely to escape the consequences of evil at home, but to plunge himself into scenes of mass destruction. Private violence and public warfare are mutually influential—and the essential sin was not to walk in the ways of Samuel.

Whatever else may be said of Jeffers' beliefs and opinions as they appear with marked consistency throughout the various poems he has written, he has gone to war in the cause of peace; and it should also be said that Jeffers' emotional fervor, his honesty, and his lack of personal vanity strongly resemble the evangelical passion of his Protestant heritage: his image of Christ is always divine. His poem to America, his "Shine, Perishing Republic," has that fervor, its eloquence, its nobility, its protest against earthly tyrants:

> And boys, be in nothing so moderate as in love of man, a
>   clever servant, insufferable master.
> There is in the trap that catches noblest spirits, that caught—
>   they say—God, when he walked on earth.

But before one considers the merits of Jeffers' best writings, one should spare breath for certain of their failures, for Jeffers is a poet of large flaws and no weaknesses—and the flaws are often easier to see than his larger merits. In the great army of

characters that his poems present to us, one has yet to discover
a wholly admirable or completely rounded human being—
the nearest approach, and her virtue is one of courage, is the
heroine of "Give Your Heart to the Hawks," a woman who
attempts to save her husband from suicide and fails. An impatient reader of Jeffers, overwhelmed, yet half attracted, and
then repelled by the scenes of overt Lesbianism in "The
Women at Point Sur" and by the sight of a mother offering
herself, half naked, to her son in "Such Counsels You Gave
to Me," would conclude that the poet kept bad company and
was himself "immoral." The same reader would also find difficulties in fully accepting Jeffers' beautiful pastoral, "The
Loving Shepherdess," which may have been written with a
memory of the Elizabethan John Fletcher's *The Faithful
Shepherdess* in mind.[4] The witless little shepherdess, dressed
in the fewest of rags, is open to all men, young and old; and it
is as though she had obeyed Sade's instructions to little girls.
Whenever in Jeffers' poetry one finds a possible echo of Sade's
doctrines, the mind, if not the blood, runs cooler. Even
Robespierre and Bonaparte, worldly men enough at the sight
of blood, and who welcomed Sade as a forthright critic of elder
institutions, were shocked and grew chilled when they read
Sade's manifestoes in the cause of sexual freedom; they were
not prudes, but they concluded that Sade's remarks were too
much of a good thing. And truly enough Sade implied too
much deliberation in the pursuits of his particular happiness;
his logic created a law for sexual lawlessness that all institutions, ancient or modern, have been forced to reject. Jeffers'
desire to deal solely with elemental passions tends to mislead

---

[4] This supposition is not so fantastic as it may seem: John Fletcher's
lyrical *The Faithful Shepherdess* was far too static in movement to be a
successful play; it is, however, an excellent poem. Its plot closely resembles
Jeffers' poem with this difference: Fletcher's shepherdess is deceived into
being promiscuous through magic worked by a sullen shepherd and she is
at last rescued and absolved by a river god.

the reader into the colder regions of hell which are a paradox of romantic agony: the reader is repelled.[5]

Another reader, equally impatient, finds something ridiculous in Jeffers' scenes of sexual violence; since no comic relief is given to the reader in Jeffers' Californian narratives, the reader is forced to supply that missing element in the progress of the story—and sex viewed from a point outside the scene itself always has a touch of the ridiculous in it; if it did not there would be no moments of relaxation in the stories that used to be told in smoking cars. It is almost gratuitous to say that Jeffers' characters lack humor, which is a flaw that Jeffers shares with Wordsworth; and in the progress of his more violent scenes of action, a need is felt for a drunken porter to cross the stage in *Macbeth*. This does not mean, however, that Jeffers lacks ability to write of drunkenness; few scenes in contemporary fiction can equal the vividness of the drunken party which is prelude to the story of "Give Your Heart to the Hawks"; in poetry, and in its own grim fashion, its veracity equals the mild, half-melancholy scene of E. A. Robinson's "Mr. Flood's Party." (Robinson, by the way, is one of the few elder American poets for whom Jeffers has expressed firm admiration.) "Such Counsels You Gave to Me" must be counted as one of Jeffers' more conspicuous failures: the bare bones of the "Oedipus complex" shine too brightly through it. As the story opens one knows only too well that the weak son is fated to poison his red-faced, hard-drinking father; since 1900 this situation has been the stock property of countless novels and plays; a sinister yet charming hero-villain disposes of a father who is overweight or a rich aunt who spikes her

---

[5] In a footnote to the pamphlet called "Frenchmen! A further effort is needed if you would be republicans!" in his *La Philosophie dans le Boudoir* (1795), Sade wrote: "The first stirring of desire that a girl feels is the moment that Nature means her to prostitute herself, and with no other consideration in mind, she should obey Nature's voice; she outrages Her laws if she resists them."

tea with whisky. But in Jeffers' case these flaws are not those of a small-minded writer or a minor poet.

3

Jeffers' merits as a poet are less well known than the flaws which I have just enumerated. From "Roan Stallion" and "Tamar" onward, Jeffers' technical contribution to twentieth-century poetry has been the mastery of alternate ten and five stress lines in narrative verse; in some of his shorter poems and in passages of some of his dramatic sequences, he employs a five and three stress variation of his narrative line. In this particular art no living poet has equaled him, and no other poet in America, from Philip Freneau to E. A. Robinson, has developed a narrative style of greater force, brilliance, and variety than his. While reading one of Jeffers' poems one never falls asleep; although there are times when his moral fervor is overweighted and has results which seem far from his stated intentions, he has never committed the greatest of all literary crimes—dullness. Among his shorter poems, his conversation pieces have contained prophecies which at the moment of publication seemed wrongheaded, probably mad, or willfully truculent. Time has proved Jeffers right more frequently than his adverse readers had thought possible; although the poem is too long for quotation here, the thoughtful reader cannot fail to be impressed by his "Woodrow Wilson (February 1924)" today. Wilson, the nearly tragic American hero, has been and still is the most difficult of all public figures to write about, yet Jeffers has succeeded in doing so. The poem's last lines, words spoken as if from Wilson's lips, indicate, however briefly, the nature of Wilson's failure:

> "This is my last
> Worst pain, the bitter enlightenment that buys peace."

Jeffers' opinions (which are less political than colored by his hatred of war, his adaptation of Nietzschean ethics, and non-churchgoing Christianity) occasioned his publishers, in a recent book of his poems, *The Double Axe,* to disclaim responsibility for them. Jeffers had strange things to say of World War II and its aftermath, which he had predicted long before they arrived; he was much too familiar with the scene to be tactful; in another ten years he will probably be found less far from the truth than the majority of his contemporaries. There has been considerable misunderstanding of Jeffers' portrait of Hitler which he included in *Be Angry at the Sun* in 1941; his Hitler was a figure not unlike Macbeth, a Macbeth who had also become the hero of a Wagnerian opera; his doom was accurately foretold; yet at the time Jeffers' poem appeared many thought that Jeffers had praised Hitler, or at least had made him seem too powerful. There is less doubt today that Jeffers' portrait needs no retouching to give it greater veracity.

Of the shorter poems, his volume *Descent to the Dead* is among his masterpieces; it includes his lines on "Shakespeare's Grave," "In the Hill at New Grange," "Ghosts in England," "Iona: The Graves of the Kings"—all memorable poems. It is impossible for an anthologist to make a neat selection of Jeffers' poems and then bind them shrewdly between the poems written by his contemporaries. It so happens that Jeffers has never written an "anthology poem";[6] he is best represented by his *Selected Poetry* which shows the range of his narratives tempered by his elegies, self-critical comments, and occasional observations; many of them may be read as footnotes to his

---

6 The perfect "anthology poem" is a showpiece of which Poe's "The Raven" and Tennyson's "May Queen" and "Crossing the Bar" were valiant examples; many minor poets seem to write for anthologies alone; and indeed, some poets like A. E. Housman are at their best when a small selection of their poems are reprinted in anthologies. With more wit and, incidentally, more truth than tact, Laura Riding and Robert Graves reviewed the practice of editing anthologies in their book, *A Pamphlet Against Anthologies.*

longer poems. Selections of his shorter poems by anthologists distort the essential qualities of his poetry.

A few quotations from Jeffers' shorter poems do show, however, how he has shocked people of rigidly fixed political opinions; from "Blind Horses" one may take the lines:

> Lenin has served the revolution
> Stalin presently begins to betray it. Why? For the sake of
>   power, the Party's power, the state's
> Power, armed power, Stalin's power, Caesarean power.

And these were printed in 1937 when many people throughout Europe and some in the United States thought differently or would have feared to make their opinions known at all. And from "Thebaid" the observation:

> How many turn back toward dreams and magic, how many
>   children
> Run home to Mother Church, Father State.

This is a statement which, like other elements in Jeffers' poetry, many may find easy to read but difficult to take; and yet it defines with Jeffers' insight and discernment a symptom of the times through which he has lived. Of the same temper are these lines from "Ave Caesar":

> We are easy to manage, a gregarious people,
> Full of sentiment, clever at mechanics, and we love our
>   luxuries.

Something of the force of Jeffers' sense of the past may be glimpsed at in these lines from "Ghosts in England":

> There was also a
> ghost of a king, his cheeks hollow as the brows
> Of an old horse, was paddling his hands in the reeds of Dozmare
>   Pool, in the shallow, in the rainy twilight,

Feeling for the hilt of a ruinous and rusted sword. But they
said
"Be patient a little, you king of shadows,
But only wait, they will waste like snow." Then Arthur left
hunting for the lost sword, he grinned and stood up
Gaunt as a wolf; but soon resumed the old labor, shaking the
reeds with his hands.

It is scarcely necessary to add that this image of King Arthur searching for Excalibur and his early moment of glory has the character of major verse. And the style in which it is written also reveals Jeffers' interlinear art of writing verse.

4

Jeffers' success in reviving Greek themes through Nietzschean and even Wagnerian interpretation has also been a source of annoyance to those who hope to read their classics in "pure" translations. The "pure" translation of Græco-Roman classics do not and cannot exist in English; and it is a truism that absolute translations of poetry from one language into another cannot be made. The best that can be hoped for is that the translator has a more than literal understanding of the poetry he translates and that he has the genius to convert his original sources into poetry in English. Jeffers' re-creations of ancient stories, particularly the plays of Euripides into English dramatic verse, have never pretended to be more than adaptations of situations, scenes, and characters. Actually, his performances are as far removed from their original sources as Shakespeare's adaptations from Plutarch's *Lives* in *Julius Caesar* and *Antony and Cleopatra,* as far as Jeffers' "Tamar" is from the second book of Samuel in the Old Testament. In his own way he has applied to ancient writings Ezra Pound's rule, "make it new." Like W. B. Yeats, Jeffers was not "a born dramatist"; as Yeats was essentially a lyric poet, so Jeffers has been a distinguished writer of contemplative and narrative verse. As Yeats's adaptation of *Oedipus at Colonus* reflects Irish seascape in a Dublin accent, so Jeffers' adaptations from the Greek are never far from the climate of the California Pacific Coast.

If Jeffers, even more than Yeats, is not a professional dramatist and is far removed from those who can be called "men of the theater," there are times when his poetry reaches high levels of dramatic power. This has long been evident in his variation of the Orestes cycle in "The Tower Beyond Tragedy"; and its concluding statement of how Orestes "climbed the tower beyond time, consciously, and cast humanity, entered the earlier fountain" (walked then, as Nietzsche would say, beyond good and evil) places the poem among the major accomplishments of our time. The same power enters his poem "At the Fall of an Age," with its story of the death of Helen on the island of Rhodes where she was worshiped as a tree-goddess, twenty years after the fall of Troy. The two speeches of Achilles' Myrmidons, risen from the dead, have all the accents of living yet timeless verse; the second speech runs as follows:

> Is there any stir in the house?
> Listen: or a cry?
> Farm-boys with spears, you sparrows
> Playing hawk, be silent.
> Splendid was life
> In the time of the heroes, the sun went helmeted, the moon
>   was maiden,
> When glory gathered on Troy, the picketed horses
> Neighed in the morning, and long live ships
> Ran on the wave like eagle-shadows on the slopes of
>   mountains.
> Then men were equal to things, the earth was beautiful, the
>   crests of heroes
> Waved as tall as the trees.
> Now all is decayed, all corrupted, all gone down,

Men move like mice under the shadows of the trees,
And the shadows of the tall dead.
The brightness of fire is dulled,
The heroes are gone.
In naked shame Agamemnon
Died of a woman.
The sun is crusted and the moon tarnished,
And Achilles has chosen peace.
Tell me, you island spearmen, you plowboy warriors,
Has anyone cried out in the dark door?
Not yet. The earth darkens.

There is nothing in poetry written during the twentieth century that is quite like this speech; few poets have written as well and the authority of the speech is unmistakable. Jean Cocteau once wrote that a true poet writes to be believed, not praised, and in these lines Jeffers' art of persuading the reader is unquestionable. Nor is he less convincing in the writing of Aphrodite's speech in his recent play, *The Cretan Woman,* a play inspired by and not a translation of Euripides:

. . . So I have come down to this place,
And will work my will. I am not the least clever of the
    powers of heaven . . .
                                        I am the goddess
        the Greeks call Aphrodite; and the Romans will call me
        Venus; the Goddess of Love. I make the orchard-trees
Flower, and bear their sweet fruit. I make the joyful birds
        to mate in the branches, I make the man
Lean to the woman. I make the huge blue tides of the ocean
        follow the moon; I make the multitude
Of the stars in the sky to love each other, and love the earth,
        Without my saving power
They would fly apart into the horror of the night. And even
        the atoms of things, the hot whirling atoms,
Would split apart: the whole world would burst apart into
        smoking dust, chaos and darkness; all life
Would gasp and perish. But love supports and preserves
        them: my saving power.

> This is my altar,
> Where men worship me. Sometimes I grant the prayers of
> those that worship me: but those who reject me
> I will certainly punish.

The quality of this speech equals the speeches in the plays of the Greek dramatists, but it is also singularly modern poetry; the quality of its language is direct and unstrained— no irrelevant effort at meaning is forced into it: the poetic nature of the speech is *there*, and for its purpose cannot be said in any other way; it is evidence enough of the genius of the man who wrote it. *The Cretan Woman* is a far more successful play to read than Jeffers' *Medea;* for his *Medea* opens with a flood of emotional speeches that cannot be sustained throughout the first act, therefore the play is top-heavy, and his readers as well as his audiences are likely to be exhausted long before the final curtain falls. Jeffers' version of Euripides' *Hippolytus* reserves its strength for the last scene and agony of Theseus; and at this conclusion, one believes that Jeffers has lost none of the mastery that he acquired thirty years ago, rather he has set himself the further task of transforming his narrative genius into writing verse for the stage, or perhaps television.

Robinson Jeffers' accomplishments and the modesty of his private life, now saddened by the death of his wife, should serve as an example to the present as well as the next generation of writers. Within the last thirty years he has made no compromise with the changing fashions of the day. For some readers Jeffers' attitude, which is not unlike the positions held by William Faulkner and W. B. Yeats, has always seemed too aristocratic. Even now I can hear someone saying, "Jeffers loves nothing but rocks and stones; I love mankind." But those who love abstract mankind too feverishly deny the rights of individual distinction and all the choices between men of good and bad, and by implication they also deny the right of the artist to be himself. Jeffers has re-established the position of the poet as one of singular dignity and courage. He is neither voiceless nor without his readers; and he is not without wisdom in seeming to await the verdict of posterity.

Wyndham Lewis:
The Artist at War
with Himself—1882–1957

OF A COMPANY WHICH INCLUDES the names of Joyce and
Pound, T. E. Hulme and T. S. Eliot, Wyndham Lewis was the
most trenchant *avant-gardist* of them all. Now that his merits
have been summed up with appropriate brightness by Hugh
Kenner, *Wyndham Lewis* (1954), and with more painstaking
seriousness by Geoffrey Wagner, *Wyndham Lewis* (1957), one
sees him as unique as ever: prophetic, yet often wrong in his
opinions, learned, yet almost righteously "self-made," hard-
headed, yet unshrewd. In the arts he practiced, fiction, painting, philosophy, criticism, journalism, he came at everything
the hard way and with distinction.

He went to Rugby and London's Slade School of art; Paris,
where he heard Bergson lecture at the Sorbonne, was his university;[1] his years from 1909 to 1928 in London can be called

---

1 Is it both irreverent and irrelevant to remember that Lewis was born on
board a British ship of which his father was captain in the Bay of Fundy?
I think not. Sometimes the accident of place of birth or the legend of it,
takes on curious meaning to what follows after in a man's career. As artist,
critic, satirist, novelist, journalist, Lewis was a "displaced" figure in British
art. After one year at Rugby (according to Mr. Wagner) and a year at the
Slade School, he spent the next six years studying painting in Munich and
in Paris; he saw something of the Netherlands and Spain—and in 1909
came back to England. Mr. Wagner is very right indeed as he observes how

by those who care for art "the Wyndham Lewis era" in Britain's capital. Like a last, phenomenally alive recruit in Cromwell's army, he conducted guerrilla warfare against British concepts of time and art, against popular brands of socialism, against ill-defined emotions and loose thinking. His assaults were carried on from the invisible ramparts he erected in Soho restaurants or behind the gates of the British Museum; he invaded whole squares of Bloomsbury, and skirted the Thames Embankment down into Chelsea, and on the edges of Kensington at Notting Hill took Ford Madox Ford's house by storm. Mr. Kenner describes it:

> Mr. Ford Madox Ford—then Hueffer—was at the top of the stairs, pink, and aghast that his privacy and his luncheon with the original of Christopher Tietjens should be invaded by a silent steeple-headed figure wearing a huge black cape. The figure mounted the stairs, saying nothing. From beneath the cape it produced and flourished crumpled rolls of manuscript, which it pressed into Ford's unnerved hands. More wads of paper appeared from beneath the hat, from inside the waistcoat, from the pockets of the long-tailed coat. Ford

---

deeply Munich's Witzblatter affected Lewis' graphic art, and as deeply as Paris, became his university. Lewis, so it then seemed, had broken through and with the tradition of British art.

The legend of his being born at sea, his self-made Continental education and his belief in both is enough to account for Lewis' sense of otherworldliness from the London world he saw, that sense which drew him toward the orbit in which T. E. Hulme, Ezra Pound, Gaudier-Brzeska, and later T. S. Eliot moved. In spite of Lewis' intellectual conversion to abstractions and cubism in the graphic arts, his painting, like so much of British paintings, held to "ideas" of painting rather than to the resources of paint and line within themselves. Anyone who looks at Lewis' self-portraits, at his portraits of his friends, Pound and Eliot, will find a center of interest in the subject, rather than in the aesthetic quality of the painting itself. However deeply Lewis was affected by European schools that came after post-impressionism, at last he remained within the tradition of British "literary" art. He, of course, never yielded to the "sweetness" of commercial art; his "ideas" rejected the "smooth," the facile, the false compromises to meet popular appeal. His failure was a failure of talent, not of critical perception of what his painting might have been—but at this point, the anti-artist in Lewis comes forward in his painting, and as a scientist might solve a problem, so Lewis' forms take on geometric contours.

numbly accepted them. All the time the figure said nothing. At last it went slowly down the stairs, without a word, and vanished.

In these singular engagements, at times accompanied by Ezra Pound, his strategy dismissed the arts of tact, and presented itself in the little magazines he edited: *Blast, Tyro* and *The Enemy;* the portraits that he painted were, more often than not, received as insults by their sitters rather than compliments; under strain of sitting for Lewis, Ronald Firbank tripped and hovered behind Lewis' shoulder to direct hopelessly, unsuccessfully, the drawing of his features upon paper. Lewis, as always, was genial enough, but decidedly intractable; he was a man of genius who possessed no talents.

In his own painting and in his criticism of modern art Lewis was a lion in wolf's clothing, his fangs bared in harsh, dark lines. From Whistler's example he evolved an ungentle art of making enemies; the last of his little magazines, *The Enemy,* revealed that debt, yet Lewis, unlike the famous American painter, was not a man of high-pitched sensibility. With matchless energy he entered and rode the violent "Machine Age" *Zeitgeist* of the early twentieth century and called it Vorticism, an explosive compound of ideas derived from Sorel, Nietzsche, and Bergson, capped with the dogmatic brilliance of Ezra Pound's young friend, T. E. Hulme. The shock was that when Lewis descended from his Vorticist chariot he showed the archetypical face of a twentieth-century Dr. Johnson, one who distrusted humanitarian ideals, yet stood for all the moral values of truculent individualism.

His first novel, *Tarr,* the writing of which was interrupted by World War I, has been imitated by younger novelists from 1918 to the present day; superficially it was another version of Bernard Shaw's early play, *The Philanderer,* in actuality, it was a nearly superhuman effort to introduce "the novel of ideas" to English readers; it proved to anyone who could think at all that the arch-Bohemian concealed a bourgeois heart and soul and that witless violence lurks in the shadows of romantic ardors. To reread it is to find it a book of more endurance than those which have attempted to improve upon it; it is among the half-dozen English novels of the present century written entirely without clichés.

But the apotheosis of the prose that Lewis so strenuously carved out as his own in *Tarr,* is in his volume of short stories, *The Wild Body;* his stern, serio-comic wit has never shown to better advantage than in his telling of the adventures of an Englishman in Brittany; the book is not merely Lewis at his best, but at least four of the stories, including "The Death of the Ankou," are among the classics of twentieth-century fiction.

Unfortunately, after writing at his best, Lewis with vigorous candor, proceeded to explain them out of existence; one does not care to deny Lewis' purpose to make his stories illustrate "the root of the comic" as he does in an essay on "The Meaning of the Wild Body," but one comes away with the conviction that Lewis, prior to 1928, wrote unevenly but far better than he knew.

The phenomenon of Wyndham Lewis involves, as Mr. Kenner suggests, an Olympian quarrel with itself; a turn of ego, untouched by vanity, which prompted him to the extremes of self-criticism, and to attempt verbal acts of satire, like *The Apes of God* and *The Childermass,* which were far beyond the resources of his prose. To be successful, Lewis' weighty fantasies in satire would have had to equal in prose Pope's *Dunciad.* Failing of that high reach, Lewis' Apes were considerably less agile than Swift's Yahoos.

From these Lewis turned to overt polemics, to unpopular political opinions, steering close to pro-Hitler sentiments and allowing the public to take his measure as a dangerous crank; the fact that he rejected socialism in all its forms was underrated and ignored, and by 1939 he was forced to write "The Hitler Cult" to correct the impression that he favored the Nazi state. Like many Europeans who had seen the horrors of

World War I he became an unwary, unguarded partisan of peace; his wars were of a moral and aesthetic order; they concerned the artist, the metaphysics of time, Western culture, and the ancient failings of human intellect. Under the stresses of public disfavor, many of his writings became powerfully dull.

In 1937 the first signs of Lewis' recovery began with his autobiography, *Blasting and Bombardiering,* a book shot through with excellent brief portraits of Joyce and Eliot and Pound— but Lewis himself is nearly made invisible as he presumed to wear the cloak of belligerent opinions. Mr. Kenner has much to say in favor of his novel *The Revenge for Love,* published in 1954, yet the book, formed with greater skill than *Tarr,* has less concentrated force than *The Wild Body.* Lewis at his best requires a small canvas in which each detail of the piece stands in relief and that is why some of the stories in *Rotting Hill,* satires of recent Britain in the toils of socialism, have more effective brilliance than his longer essays in the novel.

In 1951 word had been sent out that Wyndham Lewis had gone blind: "Milton," he said, "had his daughters; I have my dictaphone." In his manly fashion he proceeded to make the best possible use of his misfortune, to live internally, to say more to his dictaphone than he wrote in the past, and not to part with the self-lashing demon who at times all but destroyed him, yet kept him in his latter years alive. The internal war in Lewis was between the artist who made his work possible at all and the moral critic who held all works of imagination in high doubt.

In his last years, Lewis' dictaphone brought him memorable rewards. In those years came the most prophetic of his books of essays, *The Writer and The Absolute* (1952). "It is dangerous to live," he wrote, "but to write is much more so—" and with this statement he faced the situation of the serious artist. As for the writer of the twentieth century, he stated that position with equal clarity:

The writer can never hope to go of a morning into his working room with the same carefree detachment with which the man of science enters his—free to investigate our most moronic peculiarities without protest, or to devise how best to wipe us out in bulk by means of radiation or atomic fission. A relative freedom can be attained by the writer if he come in a fairly mild period. He has in many periods enjoyed it.

He glanced toward the United States and New York:

Contemporary New York might almost be regarded as a madly materialist maritime republic—carthaginian in its contempt for the writer.

There is more truth than bitterness in that remark—and an American paradox exists within it. So long as he is ignored, the American writer is "free." The present American habit of ignoring or merely patronizing poets as though they were neurotic children has given them a "freedom" far greater than poets enjoy in various capitals of Europe, including always, the Soviet Union. If in the United States, the poet compromises his gifts by yielding to the demands of "publicity," public favor, fashionable groups, he has only himself to blame.

In *The Writer and The Absolute,* Lewis clearly defined the various positions held by André Malraux, Sartre, and George Orwell. He saw Malraux, the writer, vanishing into direct political action—"escape through action," so Lewis wrote. He saw Sartre's Existentialism as twentieth-century nihilism, driving Sartre to feverish efforts to find a wide public among the bewildered, ignorant young who throng cafés, and are detached for the moment only from society—he saw Sartre drifting into a flirtatious union with Communism. From Lewis' thoroughly accurate observation of Sartre's position, further observations may be drawn. The twentieth-century nihilist with his heritage of Hegel, Marx, and Freud finds it difficult to attract sustained attention from younger readers. Younger readers, however ignorant, grow up—and the greater majority grow up and away from attitudes of adolescent disillusionment and nihilism. Abandoned elder nihilists then find themselves drawn closer and closer to the orbit of Communism. To the writer the Soviet Union has always offered the illusion of notoriety among millions of readers as a substitute for individual excellence and fame. Journalists like Sartre find this illusion irresistible—they yield to it, and are exploited by the Super State. How pitifully wrong they are is shown by the courage of Pasternak, who though living within the Soviet Union, gained his freedom as a writer in the world outside it. What Sartre lacks is courage.

Lewis' own courage and clarity of vision led him to a mature and I believe enduring estimate of Orwell's writings, and how Orwell's socialism and hasty conversion to Communism came from the springs of inverted snobbery. Lewis is right in concluding that Orwell's conversion to and later rejection of Communism (shown in his autobiographies and novels) are marred by "timely" thinking and writing, and are now outmoded. As Lewis remarks, the single proof of Orwell's integrity as artist is in his fable, *Animal Farm*, which is likely to remain as an undying reminder—a warning—of totalitarian horror.

It is appropriate that the last image of Lewis should resemble that of Tiresias—his isolation in blindness shedding light in a world with which he had never found the terms of peace. In the *avant-garde* of one age he became the seer of the next, and like Tiresias achieved a semi-Olympian authority.

The "Romantic" Heritage
in the Writings of
Dylan Thomas

THOUGH THE MERE OCCASION may seem irrelevant, I shall never forget the hour I first read a book of Dylan Thomas' verse and prose.[1] The book was Thomas' third book, *The Map of Love,* and the scene was a little bookshop in sight of the British Museum in London; the time was August of 1939. I had just come from meeting a fellow American in that very street, a little woman with rosy cheeks, tightly curled black hair beneath a hat of artificial primroses and violets; her innocent and yet bird-like eyes were wide with excitement. Without stopping for breath she told me of the Moscow-Berlin pact: "It may mean peace," she said, "and it may mean war, and of course the Russians are always strong for peace." Back at home

---

[1] After a first draft of this essay appeared in print, Dylan Thomas and the Thomas legend (in the United States) fell into the hands of "poetry exploiters"—aided by the success of Thomas reading his poems over the B.B.C. and on lecture platforms in America. Thomas knew this, and with Welsh wit remarked, "I exploit my exploiters." Of his friends, only Vernon Watkins in his *Dylan Thomas: Letters to Vernon Watkins* (1957) has served to correct an otherwise distorted picture of the poet and his writings. In the United States my essay and those by Conrad Aiken, Louis Untermeyer, and John L. Sweeney introduced Thomas' poetry to a rapidly growing circle of readers, long before the "boom."

the little woman's vocation was teaching the social sciences in a girls' college, and her war-threatened holiday in London had given her new notes on "world affairs" to carry back with her to the United States. The British Museum was already locked to visitors as though Bloomsbury gloom (with the aid of His Majesty's armed guards) had sealed its doors forever. My American lady's plump and gloved hands—the gloves were dove-gray and beautifully tailored—fluttered in half suppressed delight as though they had accidentally touched the "pulse of the world," and she, the lady, were another Pandora who at the moment had opened the fatal box. Since I had an uncheerful view of the times which to me seemed to have begun in 1914 (the date by the way of Dylan Thomas' birth) I was in no mood to share the lady's elation at the very latest "news"; such turns of history had been in "progress" for a long while, and I needed elation of another sort. I abruptly turned away from her, entered a glass-fronted shop and started to read *The Map of Love* displayed on the counter. Obviously the book could not be read at a glance, it would deserve more than several readings, and with this thought in mind, I bought it.

2

Since that afternoon in 1939 which now seems so long ago and labeled with "events" and premonitions, the Anglo-Welsh poet, Dylan Thomas, has become—and not without justice and discrimination—the most thoroughly, if not most widely, read poet of his generation in England.[2] Perhaps he is a "war

---

2 In 1946 New Directions (New York) published *The Selected Writings of Dylan Thomas*, edited and with an introduction by John L. Sweeney. The book contains forty-seven of Thomas' poems, four short stories, and the first and last chapters of *Portrait of the Artist as a Young Dog*. It is an excellently proportioned and well-modulated selection of Thomas' writings. Sweeney, in his introduction, emerges as one of the most discerning critics of contemporary verse. His prose is distinguished by wit and clarity, and no one who reads criticism for enjoyment as well as information can afford to ignore his commentary on Dylan Thomas.

poet," but I seriously doubt that kind of relevance attached to his poems and to his name—or rather it is of the same kind of relevance which attended my meeting with a teacher of social sciences in London and the purchase of *The Map of Love*. The scene out of which Dylan Thomas emerges as the central figure may be given the general title of "neoromanticism," a scene in which the later poems of W. B. Yeats and of Edith Sitwell (and it is not without grace of temperamental affinity that Miss Sitwell praised Thomas' early *25 Poems*) provided a precedent for the arrival of Dylan Thomas. Other precedents exist in the richness of Welsh poetry itself, and the annual festivals in Wales of poetry read aloud in Welsh in which the survivals of the North Druid myths are as vivid as they were a thousand years ago. Still other sources are to be found (particularly in Thomas' devotional poems, the "Vision and Prayer" cycle in *Deaths and Entrances*) in *The Temple* of George Herbert, for *The Temple* is not unknown to Welsh readers of English devotional poetry. Nor should a true "ancestor" of younger Welsh writers in England be forgotten—Arthur Machen, whose imaginative writings have gone through at least four cycles of neglect and appreciation, and are as cheerfully alive today as ever. But the "neoromantic" scene has still other figures, in which Walter de la Mare extends a heritage from Beddoes, John Clare, Poe, and Darley; and as one turns from the elder poets, the American Hart Crane and the Anglo-Irish George Barker seem to be immediate "forerunners" of the kind of lyricism that Dylan Thomas found congenial to his gifts. One should also include Henry Treece and Vernon Watkins among Thomas' immediate contemporaries, who, like Barker, reach toward a richness of expression that had been denied such poets as MacNeice and C. Day Lewis, who are often betrayed by their facility into the charms of writing "magazine verse," or colorful epithets, which may amuse or shock the eye, but fail to attach their brilliance to profound centers of human emotion or intellectual meaning. The overtly journalistic and admittedly "neoclassic" school which discovered *A Hope for Poetry* before 1939 has suffered reverses. Of that "elder" generation, W. H. Auden, by virtue of his wit and his professional skill, seems to be the sole survivor of what was "fashionable" not so many years ago.

3

The term neoromanticism does not, of course, define the specific nature of Dylan Thomas' or any other poet's poems, but it does indicate the more general atmosphere and heritage to which a poet's writings may belong; such terms as classical and romantic are always in danger of being used as weapons of abuse or as tarnished laurels, and as we come close to an actual reading of Thomas' poems, another term, symbolism, rises into view. This is all very well, but since Arthur Symons published *The Symbolic Movement in Literature* in 1899, conscious elements of symbolism and the techniques employed by the Symbolists have entered the main streams of poetry in English on both sides of the Atlantic. In respect to Thomas' poems one can say this: That which so closely resembles the technique of symbolic poetry in his poems is of the same nature that guided W. B. Yeats in his re-creations of the Celtic myth that he drew from the lives of those around him and himself, and drew also from the writings of Dr. Douglas Hyde and Standish O'Grady. In Yeats's poems the French Symbolists served as examples, as "guides," rather than "masters"—and it is safer to conclude that he did not follow them literally, but in a more active sense, attracted some features of their technique to the centers of his imaginative being. Anyone who has read the sources of a literature sprung from "the myth," and particularly the North Druid myth, soon becomes aware of their likeness to some features of so-called "modern" Symbolist poetry in English. Thomas' poems, including "The Hunchback in the Park" and "Among those Killed in the Dawn Raid was a Man Aged a

Hundred," show something of the same method that Yeats employed, a "drawing power," a fusion of "mythological" reality with individual perception. And it is to be noted that Thomas' word order often carries within it characteristically Welsh phrasing.

One index to Thomas is found in his book of autobiographical short stories, *Portrait of the Artist as a Young Dog,* and its first story, "The Peaches," is a view of things seen and heard in many of Thomas' poems. The "place" of the story is a country-side in Wales, and the "time" is childhood, literally the "time" when things are seen for the first time and at first hand. The description of "the best room" in a farm house has the very elements, the "keepings," and one almost says the "furnishings" of a number of Thomas' poems; they are the centers out of which Thomas' characteristic imagery springs and to which it returns:

> The best room smelt of moth-balls and fur and damp and dead plants and stale, sour air. Two glass cases on wooden coffin-boxes lined the window wall. You looked at the weed-grown vegetable garden through a stuffed fox's legs, over a partridge's head, along the red-paint-stained breast of a stiff wild duck. A case of china and pewter, trinkets, teeth, family brooches, stood beyond the bandy table; there was a large oil lamp on the patchwork tablecloth, a Bible with a clasp, a tall vase with a draped woman about to bathe on it, and a framed photograph of Annie, Uncle Jim, and Gwilym smiling in front of a fern-pot. On the mantlepiece were two clocks, some dogs, brass candlesticks, a shepherdess, a man in a kilt, and a tinted photograph of Annie, with high hair and her breasts coming out . . .

Another paragraph from the same story has other characteristic "keepings" which are brought to light again in Thomas' poems:

> I remembered the demon in the story, with his wings and hooks, who clung like a bat to my hair as I battled up and down Wales after a tall, wise, golden, royal girl from Swansea Convent. I tried to re-

member her true name, her proper, long, black-stockinged legs, her giggle and paper curls . . .

And still another scene from the story has a farm boy preaching a sermon from a wagon used as a pulpit. It is perhaps gratuitous to remark the well sustained prose rhythm, the shrewd yet innocent blasphemy, and the wit that is contained in the following passage:

> I sat on the hay and stared at Gwilym preaching, and heard his voice rise and crack and sink to a whisper and break into singing and Welsh and ring triumphantly and be wild and meek. The sun through a hole, shone on his praying shoulders, and he said: "O God, Thou art everywhere all the time, in the dew of the morning, in the frost of the evening, in the field and the town, in the preacher and the sinner, in the sparrow and the big buzzard. Thou canst see everything, right down deep in our hearts; Thou canst see us when the sun is gone; Thou canst see us when there aren't any stars, in the gravy blackness, in the deep, deep, deep, deep pit; Thou canst see and spy and watch us all the time, in the little black corners, in the big cowboys' prairies, under the blankets when we're snoring fast, in the terrible shadows, pitch black, pitch black; Thou canst see everything we do, in the night and the day, in the day and the night, everything, everything; Thou canst see all the time. O God mun, you're like a bloody cat."

In the above quotations one also begins to see the limitations and ranges of Thomas' vocabulary: "black" is among Thomas' favored adjectives, and the subjective associations of the "Ballad of the Longlegged Bait" (which is included in *Deaths and Entrances*) are clearly shown in the phrase, "proper, long, black-stockinged legs." The "myth" of the "Ballad" is taken from a familiar group of North Druid myths, and the "myth" or story is also implied in one of Walter de la Mare's poems. Thomas, by drawing it to the center of his own imagination— an example offered by the poems of de la Mare as well as Yeats —has made the "myth" his own. The mock-sermon provides a precedent for the "Vision and Prayer" cycle in *Deaths and*

Entrances, for blasphemy, whether in the best or worst sense, always admits the consciousness and the reality of religious being—and therefore, T. S. Eliot's "The Hippopotamus" has its place in forecasting the arrival of "Ash-Wednesday." The relationship between Thomas' prose and poetry may be shown by comparing the first passage I have quoted with a few lines from his poem, "In Memory of Ann Jones":

> Morning smack of the spade that wakes up sleep,
> Shakes a desolate boy who slits his throat
> In the dark of the coffin and shed dry leaves
> That breaks one bone to light with a judgment clout,
> After a feast of rear-stuffed time and thistles
> In a room with a stuffed fox and a stale fern.

There has been some talk of "Freudian imagery" in more than a few of Thomas' poems, and certainly Thomas has shown no fear in employing sexual imagery of which the elegy, "The Tombstone Told When She Died" is a magnificent illustration:

> The tombstone told when she died
> Her two surnames stopped me still.
> A virgin married at rest.
> She married in this pouring place,
> That I struck one day by luck,
> Before I heard in my mother's side
> Or saw in the looking-glass shell
> The rain through her cold heart speak
> And the sun killed in her face.
> More the thick stone cannot tell.
>
> Before she lay on a stranger's bed
> With a hand plunged through her hair,
> Or that rainy tongue beat back
> Through the devilish years and innocent deaths
> To the room of a secret child
> Among men later I heard it said

She cried her white-dressed limbs were bare
And her red lips were kissed black,
She wept in her pain and made mouths,
Talked and tore though her eyes smiled.

I who saw in a hurried film
Death and this mad heroine
Meet once on a mortal wall
Heard her speak through the chipped beak
Of the stone bird guarding her:
I died before bedtime came
But my womb was bellowing
And I felt with my bare fall
A blazing red harsh head tear up
And the dear floods of his hair.

Is this poem more Freudian than a poem by Blake or D. H. Lawrence or some passages that may be found in the poetry of Coleridge? I would say no more and no less. This is not to underestimate the general influence of Freud upon the poetic imagery of twentieth-century writings in both prose and verse —but the influence, as it exists in Thomas' poems, is more general and more diffuse than Thomas' relationship to the romantic tradition. And I may as well add, as a matter of opinion, that twentieth-century claims for the "modernity" of sex have been greatly exaggerated.

4

In the foregoing paragraphs I have attempted to show something of Dylan Thomas' regional identities, the charm of his highly individual imagination as well as his affinity to a larger, unevenly gifted body of neoromantic literature. Among his elders only Yeats, Edith Sitwell and Walter de la Mare are poets of greater and more mature accomplishment than he; the others, including George Barker and Henry Treece, who seem to have responded to the same impulses that have moved

Thomas (and Barker's early poems preceded Thomas' and were in print before Thomas' style had taken form), have fallen prey to the forces of "easy writing" and a tendency toward disintegration. *Death and Entrances*, was, I think, Thomas' best single book of poems published before his *Collected Poems* in 1953.

In *Death and Entrances* (1946) came the unmistakable signs of Thomas' poetic genius, his poems under the title of "Vision and Prayer," and his "Fern Hill." In the tradition of English Romantic poetry, "Fern Hill" takes its place beside Wordsworth's "Tintern Abbey." Both poems are rare in their power to re-create the spell of memory and the world of nature seen through the eyes of childhood. In this respect both convey similar emotions to the reader. The publication of his *Collected Poems* later reinforces this conclusion. In the year of his death, 1953, and in a prefatory note to his *Collected Poems*, Thomas wrote: "These poems, with all their crudities, doubts, and confusions, are written for the love of Man and in praise of God, and I'd be a damn' fool if they weren't." The statement showed his advancing maturity, his critical wit. Better than his critics he knew his flaws, but also knew his great promise of an immortality.

There was no faked piety in Thomas' prefatory note. In his *Collected Poems*, the poems of "Vision and Prayer" with their George Herbert-like verse forms, reached their conclusion in the magnificent lyric written in memory of the death of his father, which, by the way, in form is one of the few superlative examples of the French villanelle in English verse, "Do Not Go Gentle Into That Good Night." The themes of purification by fire and rebirth are implicit in "Vision and Prayer" and beyond them came the denial of spiritual death in "Do Not Go Gentle." In one sense the poem stands as Thomas' own epitaph.

During the last year of his life in the romantic confusions of his lecture tours, his violent readings of his poetry, his ill-health, his Welsh humors, he was very like an actor playing against the backdrop of a stormy night. He had succeeded in completing his role of lyric poet in a storm-ridden age of wars and threats of wars—one who was disguised one moment as an eternally boyish Welsh bard, and in the next, as Lear's prolix and witty Fool who saw and knew "the dying of the light."

The Isolation of
Isaac Rosenberg

1

We begin with high culture at the Egyptians. A land of high, profound, austere philosophy—their art expressed their priestly natures. Art went hand in hand with their religion, grave and austere. With a profound knowledge of form and perfect craftsmanship, all their energies were directed to express deity, an abstraction of simple, solemn profundity, the omnipresent spirit. Their art was angular and severe.

—from *Art*, a lecture delivered by Isaac Rosenberg in 1914.

THE YOUNG MAN WHO WROTE these lines was a poet; he had been attending classes in drawing and painting at the Slade School in London, and he was now beginning to discover that the seriousness of his intentions and the practice of them had turned from the visual arts to those of writing poetry. In fragmentary essays,[1] in letters to friends and patrons he had begun to think for himself, to observe the peculiar nature of his place in the world, for his position was peculiar: his home was in the East End of London; he was a Jew, and his education

---

[1] One of the best of the essays under the title of "Emerson" appeared seventeen years after Rosenberg's death in *Scrutiny: A Quarterly Review*, March, 1935. The essay is a brief but incisive commentary on Walt Whitman's debt to the poetry and idealism of Emerson.

at the Art School of Birkbeck College and at the Slade had been far removed from the usual British preparation at Oxford and Cambridge for the study and writing of poetry. In his letters and papers there is no evidence that he had known either D. H. Lawrence or Gaudier-Brzeska, yet among his immediate contemporaries the miner's son and the young French sculptor who moved so restlessly in "artistic circles" of London's Chelsea held positions that were analogous to his. Both Gaudier-Brzeska and Lawrence would have accepted Rosenberg's remarks upon nature: "Whatever the subject, nature is always our resort, a basis for creation. To feel and interpret nature, to project ourself beyond nature through nature, and yet convince of our faithfulness to the sensation, is imagination." But there should be no mystery as to why the three young men, so nearly of an age (Lawrence born in 1885 was Rosenberg's senior by a mere five years) did not meet. Of the three Rosenberg was the least known figure; his promise was known to Edward Marsh, to Gordon Bottomley, and to Henry Tonks, the painter, who was George Moore's old friend, and these men represented a world that stood at considerable distance from the friendship of Gaudier-Brzeska with Ezra Pound. In the *Georgian Poetry* anthologies which were modestly edited by Edward Marsh, signifying his presence only by the initials "E. M.," neither Lawrence nor Rosenberg was consistently published; Lawrence had attacked the "Georgian" standards of poetry in letters to Edward Marsh as early as 1913, and Rosenberg, who was almost as critical a contributor to the anthologies as Lawrence in his discriminations concerning the poetry of Rupert Brooke, grew friendly with Marsh after Marsh's relationship with Lawrence had turned distinctly cool. But perhaps distance between Rosenberg and his two contemporaries was that invisible distance (which cannot be measured in geographical terms) between Stepney in London's East End and the West End's semi-Bohemian Chelsea as they existed before the first World War. That distance, which was neither purely racial nor of poverty alone, but combined the qualities and unhappy relationships of both, was enough to isolate[2] and to obscure the early development of Rosenberg's talent.

The isolation in which Rosenberg wrote was not entirely to his disadvantage. Compensations are to be found in the seriousness and independence with which he regarded the important decisions he made in respect to the art he practiced, often in ill-health, until death in action while serving as a private in the British Army cut short his career on April 1, 1918. A happier situation would have modified and perhaps charmed away his conviction that "art . . . intensifies life," his conviction that "you can only talk round literature"; it was his temperament to approach questions of painting and of writing at the level of deeply rooted or radical values, and to show discontent at anything less than the standard of poems he hoped to write. In *The Collected Works of Isaac Rosenberg,* edited by Gordon Bottomley and Denys Harding, a single volume, published in London in 1937, the illustrations are half-tone reproductions of Rosenberg's paintings and drawings. Given another temperament than Rosenberg revealed in his poetry and prose, his gifts in the graphic and plastic arts would have assured him an "easy living" among those who earned a livelihood in the almost commercial art of portrait painting. At twenty-one he had mastered what now appears to have been the Slade School manner, the style of Sir William Rothenstein's popular drawings which served as illustrations to Sir William's *Men and Memories.* A chalk drawing of a blonde girl's head, the detail of a reclining figure with its eyelids closed and three self-portraits seem to have been done with happily accomplished facility. But when we turn to the "Portrait of the Artist's Father" something more than the Slade School manner shows

---

2 How keenly Rosenberg felt his isolation is shown in one of his poems, "Spiritual Isolation," a poem of Job-like character, which transcended the emotions of self-pity in its religious theme.

its hand. The figure is a conventionally placed head and shoulders in full front view against a dark background; the head is bald, the right eyebrow slightly raised over heavily lidded eyes, the pale light of the forehead and high cheek bones contrasted by the darker tones of a neatly trimmed mustache and beard, and around the throat a coarsely woven cloth held in place by the top button of a well-worn jacket. It is not a facile portrait, but one that obviously selects elements of dignity and plastic strength rather than qualities of charm and of ease in presenting its subject. It has something of the "priestly nature," "grave and austere" that Rosenberg sought for in his definition of Egyptian art; the painting was far better than others that his editors saw fit to reproduce, yet one understands why, even at their best, Rosenberg's gifts in painting could not satisfy the demands he made upon them. They fell short of being first-rate, and the fact that they did left him depressed and restless, and he would break appointments with friends and patrons rather than show them his latest paintings.

His painting was, of course, suffering from the same complaint that had afflicted the entire field of British art, a complaint which betrayed the uneasy marriage of the literary imagination with graphic forms. Exceptions to this particular disease were and still are rare and only the art of Constable and Turner, and an occasional portrait by a master of the eighteenth-century school are among them. Rosenberg struggled against what he called the "contemporary influence"; he distrusted English "charm," and he preferred "the romantic way" of Rossetti back to Pre-Raphaelite beginnings to the contemporary influence at work in British schools which so quickly reduced all adaptations of postimpressionism to illustration, to poster, and, at last, commercial art. He became all too well aware that the artist who depends on his art for his living must be an advertiser. And advertising was not what he proposed to do.

2

With these thoughts in mind Rosenberg returned to the writing of poetry. His very early poems—and some written as early as 1905—bear the marks of having been written easily and were on the level of readily acceptable magazine verse, the kind of verse which in 1905 and today, forty years later, is often published in literary magazines, and which, not unlike his drawings and sketches, could have earned him popular praise. Outwardly "formal" verse was of easy accomplishment for him, but he had been reading Keats and he had been reading Donne, and from his interests in Rossetti he turned for a short time to the poetry of Francis Thompson, a natural choice of "art . . . hand in hand with religion," since the discovery of Gerard Manley Hopkins was yet to come, Thompson best represented a late Victorian synthesis of religion and poetry in English verse. Thompson, however, was too soft, too yielding for any permanent hold upon Rosenberg's admiration, and Rosenberg had spoken with contempt of an age that regarded Keats as being "simply sensuous." Rosenberg was beginning to distinguish in his brilliant essay "On a Door Knocker" the difference between a superficial, popular romanticism and poetic reality:

> This is essentially an age of romance. . . . The philistine has be-
> come the romanticist, and the poet the philistine . . . incongruity that
> might be a Japanese fantasy. The ragged newsboy bartering news and
> information to the gentleman in the high hat. The gentleman in the
> high hat benevolently making a picture of himself for us to enjoy
> the spectacle and see, this charming young lady decked out as a
> draper's front window as if this were some merry carnival.

This paradox serves as an introduction to the ambiguous uses and qualities of a familiar object, the door knocker; the door knocker then:

> . . . is a type of prostitution, for it is sold to all men; of helplessness, for it lies where all can wreak their will on it; of power, for it sets great forces in motion; of aristocracy, for it is lordly and imperious; of democracy, for it makes no distinction between low and high; of wealth, for, like gold, it is the means of opening doors. . . .

And Rosenberg, as he sat down to write new poems that he sent in letters to his friends or printed privately in three little pamphlets, made a further observation: "Very few people say what they mean, though they may say what they think."

3

At the time of this resolution to write new poems came the war and his enlistment in the British Army. Among his ambitions was to write a play in verse, an ambition common to many "modern" poets in England, Ireland, and the United States since 1893 when Ellen Terry met with such success in a production of Tennyson's *Becket*. But whatever gifts Rosenberg possessed, they were not of the theater, nor could he relate his themes of Hebraic origin to the disciplines of writing dramatic verse. Figures of Moses, of Saul, of Lilith, and at last, a vaguely conceived and heretical Unicorn in scenes with Nubians and Amazons crowded the pages he sent to Gordon Bottomley to read. What he accomplished here was not the first draft toward writing a play, but flexibility and a fresh approach to the writing of blank verse. He had rejected smoothness in writing verse; "Regular rhythms I do not like much" he wrote to Edward Marsh, and he made the choice of seeming obscure and being "experimental." It was his purpose to write out of and within the Jewish tradition, which in itself, aside from Milton's contribution to an almost Hebraic literature in *Paradise Lost*, was an "experimental" task in English verse; the nature of Rosenberg's intention is shown in:

Through these pale cold days
What dark faces burn
Out of three thousand years,
And their wild eyes yearn,

While underneath their brows
Like waifs their spirits grope
For the pools of Hebron again—
For Lebanon's summer slope.

They leave these blond still days
In dust behind their tread
They see with living eyes
How long they have been dead.

His intentions were further realized in "Chagrin" with its first lines:

Caught still as Absalom,
Surely the air hangs
From swayless cloud-boughs,
Like hair of Absalom
Caught and hanging still.

The imagery has the same formation and is of the same world that had been seen in glimpses in an earlier and far less successful poem, "Night and Day":

Though the sun's face be on high,
Yet his fiery feet do lie
Fixed on earth. . .

The kind of promise that Rosenberg holds for those who read him is of knowing that a consistent order of poetic reality existed behind his superficial obscurities. Among its elements was his way of looking at the physical world, another was the traditional aspects of his race and its religion:

They who bowed to the Bull god
Whose wings roofed Babylon,
In endless hosts darkened
The bright-heavened Lebanon.

The following lines from another poem are of the same origin:

No blossom burst before its time,
No angel passes by the door,
But from old Chaos shoots the bough
While we grow ripe for heaven.

4

Since his death a few of Rosenberg's shorter poems have been reprinted in various anthologies which bring him back to mind as a "war poet," a survivor of the same moment and of like associations that surround the memory of Wilfred Owen; and of the two poets, Owen has remained in the more fortunate position. In latter-day revivals of Owen's name, the author of "I, too, saw God through mud—" has perhaps suffered the curse of being overrated, for like Rosenberg, his writings were cut short by death in military action in 1918. Owen was less radical, but also less fragmentary in his accomplishment than Rosenberg; in reading Owen, the reward is one of finding four or five completed poems that seem to exist for themselves alone; in reading Rosenberg, one finds the occasional line or the intractable phrase, or the presence of an isolated imagination that has evidence of life beyond the accomplishments of art. One has confidence that the coarser fibers of Rosenberg's poems were the necessary complements of what he had to say in poems that showed his hatred of war as well as the religious center of his being. His "August, 1914" is characteristic of the "war poems" that he had begun to write:

What in our lives is burnt
In the fire of this?
The heart's dear granary?
The much we shall miss?

Three lives hath one life—
Iron, honey, gold.
The gold, the honey gone—
Left is the hard and cold.

Iron are our lives
Molten right through our youth,
A burnt space through ripe fields
A fair mouth's broken tooth.

There is little self-pity in these lines, and unlike Owen,
Rosenberg with his hopes of accomplishment fixed upon the
"grave" and "austere" had no concern for

the pity of war.
The Poetry is in the pity.

Rosenberg held to a darker faith:

Moses, from whose loins I sprung,
Lit by a lamp in his blood
Ten immutable rules, a moon
For mutable lampless men.

His darkness, whether in sight of trench warfare or in
London's streets, was lighted only by such fragmentary lines as
these:

Our eyes no longer sail the tidal streets,
Nor harbor where the hours like petals float
By sensual treasures glittering through thin walls
Of women's eyes and colour's mystery.
. . . .
God gives to glisten in an angel's hair
These he has gardened, for they please his eyes.

The imperfections in these lines are obvious enough; the repetitions of "eyes" within them are not placed with the necessary skill to build the lines into a finished poem. The merits are in the phrases, "tidal streets," the "thin walls of women's eyes," and the simple use of "gardened."

If Rosenberg did not accomplish all that his poetry and prose implied, he leaves behind him a high standard of poetic responsibility. It is clear that like Owen he had broken with the popular criteria that had been accepted for poetry written before 1914. His example to younger poets of more than a generation later lies in his concern for values in poetry that dismissed immediate influences, and sought out with appropriate seriousness the central forces, which in his life were religious, of poetic imagination and character.

The Double Vision
in Pope's Poetry

To SOME READERS OF POETRY it may seem extraordinary that the poetry of Alexander Pope is again reread for pleasure—and not merely for the further search of learning. In universities, in survey courses of English literature, in research studies of eighteenth-century life and manners, Pope has always held his place, a place insured by Matthew Arnold's lecture on translating Homer. Yet the respect he earned came from the lips of middle-aged instructors and lecturers, and not from students. Even as recently as 1916 George Saintsbury with a show of boldness announced "to deny poetry to Pope is absurd," and a few years later, Lytton Strachey attempted what proved to be a brilliantly artificial defense of Pope's artificiality. At the present hour, particularly among poets and critics, a defense of Pope is gratuitous: his lines are quoted as the title of a book by a popular novelist, and the wheel of fortune, carrying with it the changes of taste and fashion, has restored Pope to his eminence. In the present revivals he has again become the poet's poet, and since such revivals often help to define the temper of the time in which we live, it is a matter of some importance to find out why. I suspect that the present generation has turned from a rediscovery of Donne to a reawakening of Pope.

To reread Pope is to admit some of his failure to command

attention from those who lived beyond the age for which he wrote. He was and still remains a topical poet, the acknowledged spokesman of London's brief Augustan Age. In his time, and for a period of nearly thirty years, everything that Pope wrote was in the highest fashion, so much so that no writer of the first half of the eighteenth century in London could claim to be more fashionable than he; and since nothing passes out of fashion more quickly than a highly modish dress in poetry, it is easy to see why the Victorians regarded Pope's poetry as scarcely more than the antiquarian's delight. To the Victorian reader, Pope's wit and polish had the same air of quaintness that today attends Broadway's productions of early plays by Bernard Shaw and Wilde's *Lady Windemere's Fan;* and what once shocked a wary audience of intellectuals and conservatives now holds its attraction as disenchanted costume drama. The serious reader of Pope's satire, the *Dunciad,* is still forced to become a student of London's Grub Street as it existed between the years of 1727 and 1743. Ezra Pound, many of whose cantos offer the same difficulties as Pope's great satire, justly complained that the *Dunciad* "needs footnotes longer than the text itself. . . . Such reading is not given for writers. It is a specialized form of archaeology."

Even in his own day adverse criticism of Pope contained charges of too much bookishness, of too many references in his verses that reflected, polished as they were, long labors pursued with the help of coffee and candlelight; and a number of these charges are still pertinent today. Pope's famous abstractions in verse which seemed to carry so much weight and said so little aroused the impatience of so friendly (to Pope at least) a critic as Dr. Johnson. It is still true that Pope was no orderly philosopher in verse, that his industrious essays on man and on criticism were as handsome, as curious, and were derived from as many sources as patchwork quilts contrived by busy-handed New England spinsters and grandmothers. All this is obvious enough to readers of Pope's verse and these limitations and defects are not likely to be removed by time.

It is natural enough, I think, that the most prominent of Pope's twentieth-century admirers is a woman, and the particular admirer, whose life of Pope has been reprinted in Penguin Books, is Edith Sitwell, and certainly she is a poet whose work cannot be charged with leaning too heavily in favor of neoclassicism. The legend of Pope's precocity, his deformed and childlike body, the brilliance of the gaze from his large eyes, seldom fails to inspire a maternal, if not matronly, affection. Behind, beyond the legend and within Pope's poetry itself lies a more profound reason for his appeal to feminine and twentieth-century sensibility. Pope's adaptation of a line from one of the Countess of Winchilsea's poems shows an understanding of and an affinity with feminine sensibility that is not accidental; his insights with respect to feminine emotion and intelligence are among the signs of his genius that have so long distinguished him from others who have chosen women as the subject of their verse. His *Eloïsa to Abelard* with its seemingly unconscious revelations of sexual imagery, in the confessions of a modest, saintly, half-innocent girl, has in it one of the triumphs of feminine character portrayal in literature. One must turn to Shakespeare's Juliet, to the fiction of Henry James and Proust, to the plays of Euripides to find its equal. Nor is his penetration less revealing in "Elegy to the Memory of an Unfortunate Lady"; and the large success of *The Rape of the Lock* owes much of its imaginative reality to the same source. Pope possessed the rare quality (which in our time was one of the gifts cherished by Virginia Woolf) of seeming to speak *for* women, of seeming to be their partisan whenever he was not their foe; and whenever the occasion of his poetry required it, he proved that he knew women slightly better than they would care to know themselves.

It is no secret that among the preoccupations of the twentieth century, clinical psychology has held and still continues to hold a highly admired place in literature. And feminine psychology as it affects and enters into the emotions of the opposite sex is among the popular themes for speculation upon the contemporary stage. At no time since the Augustan Age itself has there been so marked an interest in the niceties and details of feminine behavior as it appears in the actions of both men and women, and in that sense the present age is more than well prepared to appreciate Pope's remarkable penetration into the hidden recesses of the feminine psyche.

In his own day, Pope's understanding of feminine motives and intellect was unusual enough: Prior, Swift, Johnson, Addison, and Gay, civilized as they were, were content to express with famous bluntness distinctly masculine opinions and attitudes toward women. Compared with their less delicate perception of womankind, Pope's insights often create the illusion of his being wholly possessed by feminine discriminations and responses to the world around him. The truth is that he was not; and we need go no further than his "Epistle to Dr. Arbuthnot" and his verses to Martha Blount to prove that however far his deformity removed him from normal masculine behavior, he was not unsexed. The very circumstances of Pope's life, unhappy as they sometimes were, led to his singular creation of a double vision of nearly everything he saw and felt, overheard and thought.

Pope's deformity reserved for him a place outside the usual ambitions and pursuits of eighteenth-century London's men and women. His "long disease, my life" would not permit indulgence in the excesses of the Augustan Age, excesses in eating, in drinking, in making love, pleasures in which so many of his contemporaries took delight. His father's conversion to the Roman Church cut short all prospects of the son's political ambitions, should he have had them—and in return for these losses, came a double vision of the world which passed before his eyes. By temperament and training Pope was scarcely one to claim the poet's prerogative as seer, yet his peculiar relationship to the world around him—the state of being of the world, and yet out of it (a position not unlike that of the majority of twentieth-century poets)—helped to sustain the double vision he enjoyed and therefore shielded the gifts which gave him insights reaching beyond the limitations of place and time.

Perhaps there is no better illustration of Pope's success in piercing the walls of masculine prejudice and to move at ease behind the masks of human sentiment than that which enters the descriptive passages of his epistle to Martha Blount; he speaks for her as well as for himself; and all she has to say is in her actions, not her words:

> She went, to plain-work, and to purling brooks,
> Old fashion'd halls, dull Aunts, and croaking rooks;
> She went from Op'ra, Park, Assembly, Play,
> To morning-walks, and pray'rs three hours a day;
> To part her time 'twixt reading and bohea;
> To muse and spill her solitary tea;
> Or o'er cold coffee trifle with her spoon,
> Count the slow clock, and dine exact at noon;
> Divert her eyes with pictures in the fire,
> Hum half a tune, tell stories to the squire;

As in the best of all Pope's writings, there is no mistaking the surface meaning of these lines; it is an excellent description of boredom at a country seat, and that is the general intention of this passage in the poem. Yet as one rereads it the subtle portrait of a particular bored lady enters the scene; decorum covers her inward restlessness; she spills her tea, she trifles with her spoon, counts the slow clock—and the portrait takes on all the finer shadings of repressed emotion. Later on in the poem we learn that she is not attracted by the Squire who "Makes love with nods and knees beneath a table,—" and the implication is that she has become used to, has formed a taste for, talk in urban and witty company and has the brains to share it. The poem is, of course, a love letter in verse, and

Pope, unlike many a writer before and after him, does not neglect (within the poem itself) the object of his affections. If he does not tell us the color of the lady's hair and eyes, nor speak precisely of her voice and figure, he leaves no doubt as to what her actions are, and how she thought and felt—and this is the greatest compliment of all possible tributes to her character.

In the creation of Pope's particular gift of a double vision some acknowledgment is due to the household in which the poet spent his childhood. The elder Alexander Pope was a retired linen merchant of comfortable means, and after his conversion to the Roman Church, he married within the small circle that held to "the old religion," which included then as it does today, descendants of the elder British gentry. The Pope household thrived decorously within a group that had learned to give up political ambitions and civil privileges; it consciously avoided persecution and made the most of British tolerance that showed a smiling aspect to successful and respectable members of the merchant class. Even among the smaller landed gentry, doors were left slightly ajar to modest, respectable merchants like the elder Pope who had the means to buy a little estate on the edge of Windsor Forest.

The true concern of the Pope household revolved around the education of the precocious and sickly boy; barred from public schools and universities because of the elder Pope's religious faith, barred from regular attendance at Catholic schools because of his own ill-health, the poet was fortunate to find in his sympathetic father a first critic of his verse. Pope learned the rudiments (but scarcely more) of Greek and Latin at home, and though he maintained a love of books and an outward show of learning, he had little enough of the academic temperament acquired later in his century by Thomas Gray. What scholarship Pope possessed remained untouched by the vice of pedantry, and fortunately his gifts were free of recurrent premonitions of sterility which so often attend the fears of those who write within the uncharmed circles of academic life.

Like many who are forced by ill-health to be a spectator of the world, Pope's curiosity seldom failed to be aroused by active scenes of urban life, and another aspect of his double vision is distinctly visual and shuttles between the library indoors, suburban woods and meadows, and the interior of houses in the town.

The double vision of Pope's world moved readily from views of Windsor Forest to London's coffee houses, and the contemplative child, fresh from his imitations of Chaucer and Spenser and exercises in translating Ovid, read both with precocious brilliance. Many years later in writing lines to his friend John Gay from Twickenham, the all-seeing childlike eye fixes its long gaze upon a pastoral detail of a hunting park or forest:

> So the struck deer in some sequestered part
> Lies down to die, the arrow in his heart;
> There stretched unseen in coverts hid from day,
> Bleeds drop by drop; and pants his life away.

And from another poem one finds these lines:

> More subtle web Arachne cannot spin,
> Nor the fine nets, which oft we woven see
> Of scorched dew, do not th'air more lightly flee.

The poet who cannot ride to hunt discovers his sentiment on the side of the struck deer; and the bright, sharp, near-sighted gaze selects an image, which is almost invisible, of scorched dew. Neither view is one that a countryman (and certainly not a hard-riding country squire) is likely to carry in his mind, and one need not press the point that both reflect an urban sensibility. Pope's town scenes are of rooms and halls, of which major examples may be drawn from *The Rape of the Lock,* and beyond these the double vision shifts from eye to ear; one overhears talk crowded with activity, gossip through which names float, and words pour from the coffee house, boudoir, council chamber, and narrow street: the sounds are often vigorous and sometimes shrill and loud; they are of the double vision speaking in the voice of the snake with a forked or double tongue:

> Know, there are Words, and Spells, which can control
> Between the fits this Fever of the soul:
> Know, there are Rhymes, which fresh and fresh apply'd
> Will cure the arrant'st Puppy of his Pride.
> Be furious, envious, slothful, mad, or drunk,
> Slave to a Wife, or Vassal to a Punk,
> A Switz, a High-dutch, or a Low-dutch Bear;
> All that we ask is but a patient Ear.

In his *Moral Essays* there is still another kind of portrait of those who walk the town:

> Boastful and rough, your first Son is a Squire
> The next a Tradesman, meek, and much a liar;
> Tom struts a Soldier, open, bold and brave;
> Will sneaks a Scriv'ner, an exceeding knave:
> Is he a Churchman? then he's fond of pow'r:
> A quaker? sly: A Presbyterian? sour:
> A smart Free-thinker? all things in an hour.
>   Ask men's Opinions: Scoto now shall tell
> How Trade increases, and the World goes well;
> Strike off his Pension, by the setting sun,
> And Britain, if not Europe, is undone.
>   That gay Free-thinker, a fine talker once,
> What turns him now a stupid silent dunce?
> Some God or Spirit he has lately found:
> Or chanc'd to meet a Minister that frown'd.

The passage brings to light some speculation as to the nature of Pope's religious faith: and was the double vision there? Since his father was a convert to that faith, Pope had no need to make religious vows in print. His religion was the private conviction of his household and it also included that of Martha Blount's. His position upheld and not without the use of reason, a conservative Christian standard of behavior, and what he gathered from his faith was an air of strict detachment in looking at the follies of British Protestant mankind. His opinions of the Quaker, Presbyterian, and Free-thinker were those that could be accepted and shared by any worldly Londoner of the day, yet it is perhaps a matter of interest to discover that members of his own faith were excluded in his list. In general Pope was content to say: "presume not God to scan; / the proper study of Mankind is Man," and this statement probably expresses all that he wished the world to know of his religious faith. In worldly matters his double vision permitted rays of skepticism to illuminate everything that was not reserved for the working of God's will.

Of all his writings the twentieth-century reader of Pope's verse is best prepared to understand the technical force and skill of the "Epistle to Dr. Arbuthnot," and familiar as the piece may be, it still yields fresh claims upon our attention. Since the arrivals of Thomas Hardy and E. A. Robinson within the scope of reading poetry, there have been many successful innovations in writing conversational verse, and the range extends from many sources and in great variety from Frost, Pound, and Eliot to William Carlos Williams, E. E. Cummings, and Robinson Jeffers. To the contemporary eye and ear, Pope's famous "Epistle" is closer to our taste than passages of equal length from Tennyson and Longfellow— which is to say we feel the presence of poetry in Pope's "Epistle" with the same conviction that Victorian readers were certain that the "Epistle" was no more than admirably brilliant verse.

In a contemporary reading of the "Epistle," the piece becomes in the guise of topical satire, spoken to a friend, Pope's autobiography, his *ars poetica* and epitaph,—and more than that, the "rocking horses" of his couplets, if not entirely stilled, have given way to the sound of human voices, Pope's and Arbuthnot's within a room. It is always the kind of poetry that is not declaimed, and to be heard correctly and understood, should be spoken without too many stresses upon its rhymes.

Pope's biographers and commentators have long discarded the literal truthfulness of what he had to say in his "Epistle" and they have been wary of assuming that unguarded confessions poured from his lips. But the occasion of writing a prologue to his satires from Horace was one that allowed him to tell essential truths about himself; he was at the height of his fame and had under his control the full resources of his skill, his art, his genius; he could well afford to permit the world to see within and between the lines he wrote the conflicts of his mind and heart. The "Epistle" was his proof that he had put into practice his instruction, "Know thyself," and that he also possessed the wit and strength of mind to purge self-pity from his lines. After his confession that his life was a "long disease," he pointed to his notoriety, his fame, and then permitted himself the luxury (which is no less revealing) of releasing the bitterest and most artful of his libels upon Lord Hervey. Anyone who reads between his Sporus passage cannot waste tears of pity over Pope; his success is far too evident, the triumph of his art and will are both too overwhelming and assured.

In his excursion into autobiography was it Pope who paved the way for Wordsworth's great poem, *The Prelude,* as well as Byron's *Don Juan?* There is, I think, the sight of truth in what may seem to be a broad speculation. We know how much Byron owed to Pope and how readily he acknowledged his debt to him; and we know that Wordsworth's blank verse in *The Prelude* bears an honest kinship to the paragraphs of verse in Milton's *Paradise Lost.* We know that Wordsworth's conception of writing conversational verse was of a very different mind, temperament, accent and rhythm than any rules that Pope had held to in making his voice heard. In fact almost any meeting of Pope and Wordsworth on common ground is like the meeting of opposites where both extremes incontinently meet. Yet it is likely that we have forgotten that Wordsworth read Pope with care enough to oppose him with great success, and that most of the Romantics paid tribute to Pope's presence on the horizon that they had left behind them. Among these Robert Burns may seem to be a strange example, all the more so because his "Cotter's Saturday Night" illustrates how dull a merely correct imitation of Pope's couplets can be. Yet Burns's emulation of Pope (and Burns turned to Pope with all the humility of going to a master) had extremely fortunate results; Pope's "The Challenge, A Court Ballad," points the way:

> To one fair lady out of Court,
>   And two fair ladies in,
> Who think the Turk and Pope a sport,
>   And wit and love no sin!
> Come, these soft lines, with nothing stiff in,
> To Bellenden, Lepell and Griffin.
>   With a fa, la, la.
> . . . .
> But should you catch the prudish itch,
>   And each become a coward,
> Bring sometimes with you lady Rich,
>   And sometimes mistress Howard;
> For virgins, to keep chaste, must go
> Abroad with such as are not so.
>   With a fa, la, la.

The ease and lightness of these lines is a step in the direction of Burns's "The Jolly Beggars"; and in his own way Burns emulated the conversational vigor of the "Epistle to Dr. Arbuthnot" in his own epistles and satires. But to return to Wordsworth's masterpiece, *The Prelude,* and its probable, though well concealed, relationship to Pope's "Epistle": If we admit that the "Epistle" is a poet's testament, written at the height of his powers, and is so balanced in its structure that all its parts combine to show the growth of a poet's mind, we have an excellent precedent for Wordsworth's major poem. There can be little doubt that the "Epistle," at the very least, was intended to be and become a backward-looking survey of Pope's life and work,—if not, why did he take the trouble to mention his earlier writings within it, why did he dwell on Lord Hervey who was so intimately associated with Pope's long-lived quarrel with Lady Mary Wortley Montague? It was not Pope's habit to write poems without a well deliberated purpose in his mind.

Although it may seem strange to credit a conscious neo-classicist like Pope with certain qualities that create a precedent for well-known elements in romantic poetry (and the personal testament in verse is one), a rereading of Pope's *Pastorals* brings us to the obvious conclusion that if a poet actually writes poetry, the naming of schools and movements become irrelevant; only the lesser and half-gifted poets are sustained by the naming of groups and classroom definitions. Pope, who seldom saw a classroom in his life, tends to escape the formulas of usual definitions for neoclassical verse. Like the romantics who came after him Pope in his youth read Edmund Spenser, and learned from him the finest, the most delicately written and heard lyric strains in English poetry; Pope made his own adaptation of Spenser's music (with unclaimed, unsuspected originality) to his chosen form of the heroic couplet. His pastoral "Autumn" has two refrains, "Go, gentle gales," and "Resound, ye hills;" the exercise is admittedly youthful and experimental, yet how fresh, how nearly "romantic" its images and music are today:

> Go, gentle gales, and bear my sighs away!
> Curs'd be the fields that cause my Delia stay!
> Fade ev'ry blossom, wither ev'ry tree,

Die ev'ry flower, and perish all but she!
What have I said? Where'er my Delia flies,
Let Spring attend, and sudden flowers arise!
Let op'ning roses knotted oaks adorn,
And liquid amber drop from ev'ry thorn.

Even in these lines the curious insight of a double vision are in evidence; probably the inspiration behind them was no more than the delight of metrical invention and exercise; his Delia is unreal enough and has no relation to his Eloïsa and the fears and distractions of his "Unfortunate Lady," yet images of life, perhaps subconsciously conceived and drawn from an exact observation of natural forms close the passage just before the refrain begins again.

One of the survivals of Pope's legend in contemporary literature occurs in the last of Dylan Thomas' sketches in *The Portrait of the Artist as a Young Dog*. The scene is at a seaside resort, and lines from Tennyson's "Maud" have just been read. Someone remarks in the dialogue which follows:

'My grandfather remembers seeing Lord Tennyson, he was a little man with a hump.'
'No, he was tall and he had long hair and a beard.'
'Did you ever see him?'
'I wasn't born then.'
'My grandfather saw him. He had a hump.'
'Not Alfred Tennyson.'
'Lord Alfred Tennyson was a little man with a hump.'
'It couldn't have been the same Tennyson.'
'You've got the wrong Tennyson, this was the famous poet with a hump.'

Needless to say, Thomas' setting among drinking men and girls for Pope's arrival is shamelessly romantic; it is a queer place to find him; but the sight of his figure and the sound of his voice, whenever we choose to rediscover them within his poetry, are as much alive today as they were in England's Augustan Age.

The Nocturnal Traveller:
Walter De La Mare

1

THE POETRY AND PROSE OF Walter de la Mare lean over a bridge of years from the last century into our own. Among some of the things of which his writings tell us are the peculiar haunting memories that the environment of the nineteenth-century still holds. Twenty years ago, it was easy to insist that we had thoroughly outgrown, or had outrun, even the memory of late nineteenth-century decor; of course we had not; we were still possessed, half-sleeping in our dreams, of mechanical Speed and Progress.

As for de la Mare, he continued to write, in the same fashion he had made his own, stories and rhymes for children, two novels, *The Memoirs of a Midget, The Return,* books of short stories, poems—and he appeared to devote his leisure moments to the making of anthologies, collections of verse and prose which did not in the least resemble the usual piecing together of other men's wits and genius, but were books of imaginative insight and discovery. It had become de la Mare's way to approach his readers by an entrance through the nursery (a popular path, if one is at all successful—and a very dangerous one) in his anthologies. The path is clear in his *Come Hither,* a collection of rhymes, poems, and verses, so arranged as to introduce children to the reading of poetry. That was its thoroughly innocent disguise; it did not pretend to teach children how to read poetry, or to find a moral hidden within a poem, or how to find a meaning that a poem might contain. The concealed plot of the book was to awaken whatever is meant by the word "imagination." I don't know how many people have given the book to children, or read it aloud to them; I suspect that many have intended to make a gift of it to a child and then kept it themselves, or presented it to older children than the child they originally had in mind; it is a book in which imagination remains unglossed—for to people who have no poetic imagination, "imagination" keeps children awake at night and guides them in the telling of frightfully neurotic lies.

I have spoken of the dangers de la Mare has run in approaching his readers through the doors of the nursery, and his writings are distinctly affected by that approach. Others have entered through the same door: Edward Lear, Lewis Carroll, and, with measurable damage, so have Robert Louis Stevenson and J. M. Barrie. In the cases of Lear and Lewis Carroll the mask of childhood offered an appropriate release for the genius of the writers behind the mask, yet neither men, in spite of the popular success of their books for children, were professional writers. They were not afflicted by the professional need to write for children, which can become a great and crippling affliction. The convention of writing of and for children did not injure Stevenson's *A Child's Garden of Verses,* nor did it mar the adventurous wanderings toward *Treasure Island;* even *Dr. Jekyll and Mr. Hyde,* the downward look into the mystery of dual personality and the play of forces of good and evil within it, remained unharmed by the convention of childhood memories, insights, desires. *Dr. Jekyll and Mr. Hyde,* founded on the famous case of Deacon Brodie of Edinburgh, kept Stevenson within the charmed circle of his childhood memories—but when his perception revealed an identity other than that which childhood memory permitted, the convention of writing stories for Victorian boys and girls crippled his hand—and the result was an abortive masterpiece, *The Master of Ballantrae*. Stevenson feared to give his readers an adult answer to his final variation of the good vs. evil theme. The same fears, the same curse afflicted J. M. Barrie's *Peter Pan*. The truth that Barrie so valiantly discovered, the desire for eternal sexless youth, failed of its translation into other than sentimental terms; a frightening charm still permeates the movement of the play, a charm that remains unpurged of its essential fears and premonitions of disaster.

These are the dangers that de la Mare chose to run, and at his second best he is not quite free of them. One convention of the nursery is charm; and the second best invades the verses of "Nod." Charm is there:

> His drowsy flock streams on before him,
>   Their fleece charged with gold,
> To where the sun's last beam leans low
>   On Nod the shepherd's fold.
> . . . .
> His lambs outnumber a noon's roses,
>   Yet, when night's shadows fall,
> His blind old sheep-dog, Slumber-soon,
>   Misses not one of all.

The musical art that went into the making of these two stanzas is nearly flawless; there is a rocking movement in the lines, and the line falls to rest, yet the result is oversweet and coy, and the sign of danger is in the name of the shepherd's dog, "Slumber-soon." All usual expectations are gratified; everything is safely, noiselessly at rest—but everything is a shade too artfully, too safely said. One does not quite believe it; it is too professional, too pat. It is when de la Mare's charm has more than itself to recommend it that its internal strength endures beyond its artfulness. Within the blue and white China walls of the nursery, a good Dr. Jekyll is in need of the evil and crooked shadow of a Mr. Hyde behind him. In that shadow the secret of de la Mare's magic lies. The shadow is behind all things within the nursery, behind all green and gray stone garden walls, and in that shadow is concealed much of what de la Mare has to say. He has written somewhere that it is the meaning that exists, not in words, but *between* them which is so important, so difficult to make clear. And for the lyric poet, more than half the meaning of a poem is in its music:

> And when I crumble who will remember
> That lady of the West country?

Disassociated from the rest of the line, the word "crumble" is almost ridiculous, but to hear its association with "remember" and to associate it with the wearing away of a headstone in a churchyard, is to understand that an act of magic has been performed, and it is the kind of felicity of which de la Mare is a master. I doubt whether these two lines would make sense in any other language than that of English.

2

And what of the stories that de la Mare has written? His excellence is to be found in four of them: "Seaton's Aunt," "Miss Duveen," "The Three Friends," "The Green Room." In three of them, the spell exerted by another century than ours casts its shadow across the page; it haunts each story. That spell is what Max Beerbohm has caught in his cheerfully wry caricature of him sitting in a Victorian parlor at the footstool of a formidable maiden lady, but it is also the same aspect of de la Mare's prose writings that places them in the genre of the short stories of Sheridan La Fanu, whose "In a Glass Darkly" has been recently revived and reprinted, whose *Uncle Silas* has received the respect and admiration of Elizabeth Bowen. It is the genre of which James's *The Turn of the Screw* is a famous illustration; the best of de la Mare's stories depend upon the intense, and subtle perceptions of concealed guilt, ambitions, desires; they are revelations of the hidden will to power that so often corrodes the mind, and love is transformed into the desire to possess wholly the psyche of the loved one. It has been de la Mare's achievement in this genre to arrive upon the scene with a deceptively innocent eye: in telling the story of poor Seaton devoured by an implacable Aunt, he has the air of calmly reciting a fragment of schoolboy memoirs, and in "Miss Duveen" there is the figure of a lonely child, housed with an unsympathetic grandmother, who finds an affinity with the unloved old maid, a neighbor, Miss Duveen. Miss Duveen has lost her wits and knows she has, but she has retained her moments of intuitive knowledge which are shared by the lonely boy. Miss Duveen's ancient sins are sins of family pride and vanity—and the sin of maidenly diffidence, the most delicate and insidious sin of all, which is so often called "modesty" and which grew like a weed in many green and rainswept Victorian gardens. As the boy grows older he sees Miss Duveen drifting toward madness:

> I began to see we were ridiculous friends, especially as she came now in ever dingier and absurder clothes. She even looked hungry, and not quite clean, as well as ill; and she talked more to her phantoms than to me when once we met.

When the boy learns that Miss Duveen's friends have been compelled to put her away, there were no tears:

> But I know now that the news, in spite of a vague sorrow, greatly relieved me. I should be at ease in the garden again, came the thought—no longer fear to look ridiculous, and grow hot when our neighbour was mentioned, or be saddled with her company beside the stream.

This is the end of an early friendship and the end of the story, and I quote directly from it to show how simply, firmly, precisely de la Mare purges "Miss Duveen" of all false sentiment and how securely he steps out of the trap where lesser writers however honestly inspired, have lost their poise.

Of the three stories in which the shadow of *time past* falls across the page, "The Green Room" is an obvious tour de force, yet it is of a kind that could be practised only by a poet of de la Mare's extraordinary skill in making verse that serves his purpose in defining the characters of an inept, self-centered poetess and her posthumous, well intentioned, naive young editor. A less perceptive, less artful writer than de la Mare would have been content to make his ghostly, romantic heroine no more than an outrageously bad poet, for in the writing of this story the temptation is to make her the object of satire, which would have destroyed the power she held over her editor and completely alienated the best of his good intentions. For de la Mare's purpose her verse must be good enough to deceive the young, the enthusiastic reader who thinks he is reading poetry when he is reading the effusions of a strong-willed, self-possessed young woman—her verses have the attractions of a lady in love and in distress and of lyric facility, if not art, that so often pass for poetry among those who do not read poetry too often or too well. This the kind of mock-poetic presence which in every age makes its appearance somewhere either in verse or fiction on a respectable publisher's list and which ten years later fills the darker shelves of the secondhand bookseller. In this case the ghost happens to be of early nineteenth-century origins, one who is very nearly another Emily Brontë, but is not, yet is powerful enough to haunt the imagination of the editor who discovers her manuscript in the library of a rare book shop; his encounter with it has all the force and, of course, all the illusion of an actual love affair.

One can read into this story several ethical conclusions: one can say that good intentions are of little value to an editor or critic, that vague young men are too easily possessed by strong-willed young women, that one should distinguish between the ghost of reality and reality itself, that the projection of a self-centered personality must not be mistaken for literary art—but it is among the rules of de la Mare's art to stress none of these; these conclusions are left to the will and temperament of the reader; it is enough for de la Mare to evoke the dual presence of unearthly and worldly reality, and despite the charms of his external gifts in telling a story, to reveal the flaws, not without a suggestion of evil, which are concealed within human action and emotion.

The best key to the central meaning, so artfully hidden in a number of de la Mare's stories, is found in one of the shortest of them all, "The Three Friends," in which two elderly men discuss the problem of an "after-life" and personal immortality. The comic scene includes a friendly barmaid. Of worldly being Mr. Eaves remarks:

> I might change in a score of ways . . . I might fall ill . . . I might come into some money; marry again. God bless me, I might *die!* But there, that is in the "after-life"; that's all over; no escape; nothing. I can't even die. I'm just meself, Miss Lacey; Sully, old friend. Just meself for ever and ever . . . it's just what Mr. Sully says . . . it's my sentence. Eh, Sully? wasn't that it? My sentence?
>
> Sentence! Oh, no! You! cried Miss Lacey . . . You've never done no harm, Mr. Eaves!

It is not my intention to transform de la Mare into an Existentialist philosopher, yet it is of some moment that his Mr. Eaves conceives of an immortality as "no escape" from what he is; "it isn't what you do . . . It's what you are"; which observation was arrived at long before Jean-Paul Sartre wrote *No Exit.* There is no comfort in the best writings of de la Mare for soft-hearted children and their parents; if and when he is whimsical, whatever exists between his lines, or on the other side of a green tinted mirror of the world, has in it somewhere the chill of ice, or the rational touch of snow.

3

As one returns from de la Mare's stories to his poems, it is no more than the necessary step from one form of writing to another; the qualities of both fancy and imagination remain the same, and no writer of his day, with the possible exception of W. B. Yeats, has relied so completely upon the resources of imaginative power. In this sense, as well as in other affinities, de la Mare is a Romantic poet in the best European tradition. It is an association that permits him to measure his standards for lyric verse by the writings of Poe, Beddoes, and Darley as well as those of Robert Herrick, Thomas Campion, and Thomas Hardy; his coolness, his "reason," has less affinity with the strictly neoclassic poets than with the "sons of Ben Jonson," who had little in common with the sterner virtues of either Milton or Dryden, and whose conception of classical form was not restricted by varieties of blank verse and the heroic couplet.

All this is another way of saying that de la Mare is a traditional lyric poet "with a difference"; that in England today and with Edith Sitwell and Dylan Thomas he fills the vacuum created by the failure of younger poets to grow beyond the promises of talent and the writing of further essays on Ezra Pound and T. S. Eliot; this is not to belittle Eliot's stature as a poet nor to forget his tribute written in memorable verse to de la Mare,[1] but to define, as best I can, the peculiar eminence

---

1 Part of which is:

> When the familiar scene is suddenly strange
> Or the well known is what we have yet to learn
> And two worlds meet, and interest, and change;

which de la Mare's poetry holds in England, and the sense of relief and of assurance that the public feels in reading it. Those who read de la Mare's poems are confident that they are reading poetry, verse and rhyme are there; read aloud, the poems sound like poems; they look like poems; they seem familiar to the ear and eye. This particular kind of public confidence has given de la Mare's poetry the outward semblance of being a safe choice for reading aloud to children, to one's near relatives, or to one's self.

It is on a second or third reading of the poems that a sense of difference arrives; the poems seem so effortless, so "right," so rhymed with ease that what de la Mare is actually saying has a way of sliding beneath the surface of his lines; one almost expects a platitude, or at best a well-worn sentiment, but what one finds is decidedly something else, of which the poem called "Away" (in *Collected Poems*) is a memorable choice and from which after a second reading, it is difficult to dislodge its meaning and music from one's ear and mind:

When cats are maddened in the moonlight dance,
Dogs cower, flitter bats, and owls range
At the witches' sabbath of the maiden aunts;

When the nocurnal traveller can arouse
No sleeper by his call; or when by chance
An empty face peers from an empty house;

By whom, and by what means, was this designed?
The whispered incantation which allows
Free passage to the phantoms of the mind?

By you; by those deceptive cadences
Wherewith the common measure is refined,
By conscious art practised with natural ease;

By the delicate, invisible web you wove—
The inexplicable mystery of sound.

From *Tribute to Walter de la Mare: on His Seventy-fifth Birthday*. London: Faber and Faber, 1948.

There is no sorrow
Time heals never;
No loss, betrayal,
Beyond repair.
Balm for the soul, then,
Though grave shall sever
Lover from loved
And all they share;
See, the sweet sun shines,
The shower is over,
Flowers preen their beauty,
The day how fair!

Brood not too closely
On love, or duty;
Friends long forgotten
May wait you where
Life with death
Brings all to an issue;
None will long mourn for you,
Pray for you, miss you,
Your place left vacant,
You not there.

The sentiment of the second stanza is not the usual conclusion to the lines which precede it; on first reading, one is caught up, shielded and reassured by the general tone of optimism which gilds the surface of the opening stanza; it contains but a single warning of what is to follow: "Though grave shall sever/Lover from loved/And all they share"; one is also caught up in the delights of hearing de la Mare's play of inner rhymes, so that the reversal of sentiment from easy consolation and day-lit brightness to a dark speculation falls as a surprise; the poem is no longer easy and familiar.

More delicate, yet more adventurous in form, and more precise in the placing of separate word and phrase is "Autumn" (in *Collected Poems*):

There is a wind where the rose was;
Cold rain where swept grass was;
   And clouds like sheep
   Stream o'er the steep
Grey skies where the lark was.

Nought gold where your hair was;
Nought where your hand was;
   But phantom, forlorn,
   Beneath the thorn,
Your ghost where your face was.

Sad winds where your voice was;
Tears, tears where my heart was;
   And ever with me,
   Child, ever with me,
Silence where hope was.

The progress from the usual observation to the particulars of deeper feeling and sentiment carries the meaning of both poems; both poems show, honorably enough, a philosophic debt to Hardy; one recalls Hardy's "The Garden Seat," and "Transformations." The debt is strictly philosophic and not a literal exchange of "influences" at work between two poets. Hardy's view of nature held for its precedent Wordsworth's pantheism, yet it was a face of nature transformed by what Hardy called a "plethoric growth of knowledge simultaneously with the stunting of wisdom." To Hardy the turn of the nineteenth century into the twentieth and the events of World War I brought the threat of a "new Dark Age," which, as he phrased it, showed in "The barbarization of taste" and "the unabashed cultivation of selfishness in all classes." The phrasing of Hardy's criticism carries the accents of an elderly Victorian, but the sense of what he said is not without a note of prophecy; his view of nature in "The Last Chrysanthemum" "is but one mask of many worn/By the Great Face Behind," and the transformation of human energy—a more particular, yet darker view than Wordsworth's—entered Hardy's trees and grasses.

Hardy's rule for the recapturing of wisdom included a recognition of a psychic relationship of men and women to other forms of life, even to inanimate things and places, and from this philosophic root de la Mare has made his own field, "pasture" one almost says, his world of psychological and metaphysical reality.

In the creation of his field of vision, his view is singular and minute in detail, an independent view that remains unconcerned with fashions in writing verse and one that has been sustained since the publication of his first book of poems, his *Songs of Childhood.* As in his prose, so in his poems, he does not speak to teach, but to reveal: and this distinction is, I believe, an important one. It is true that some of his stories are as delicately poised, as penetrating, as *revealing* as some of the shorter writings of Henry James; their psychological subtlety is no less effective, their art no less in evidence; they lack only the strong fibers of an ethical, a moral fabric that sustain the inner meanings as well as the larger aspects of James's novels. De la Mare's relationship to James and Hardy may be compared to Robert Herrick's relationships to Donne and Ben Jonson; one cannot claim for Herrick the metaphysical powers of Donne, nor the large worldliness of Jonson's wit, yet Herrick, on his occasions, wrote with great excellence "Rex Tragicus, or Christ Going to His Cross" and the complex "Corinna's going a Maying," one of the masterpieces of English verse.

In de la Mare's poetry wit is allied to revelation; it appears in the lines of one of his childhood rhymes, his "Poor Jim Jay/(Who) Got stuck fast/In Yesterday," which resolves itself into a metaphysic of time and space. And why does de la Mare place his childhood rhymes so prominently within his field of vision? The first answer should be that he enjoys the wit of doing so, the wit of revealing a metaphysic where it is least expected, but the second answer, which lies behind it, is of profound relevance to the central meaning of more than half his poems. In giving a lecture at the Rugby School in 1919, de la Mare said, "A child, a visionary, lives in eternity; a man in time, a boy—sheer youthfulness—in the moment." Among his later poems, under the title of "The Chart" (in *Winged Chariot and Other Poems*), are these four lines:

> That grave small face, but twelve hours here,
> Maps secrets larger than the seas',
> In hieroglyphics more austere,
> And older far than Rameses'.

To be childish in the sense that de la Mare presents childhood vision is to exist before temporal consciousness distorts the knowledgable world; his is a clarity of vision that Lewis Carroll shared in his adventures with Alice, of things seen at the level of a grass blade. It is de la Mare's poetic conceit that the antiquities, Egyptian or Druid, including Stonehenge and the recent ruins of World War II, which brood over England today, contribute to a sense of the past. This is not easy to define, nor is a literal interpretation of the landscape within his poems desirable; yet no recent poem of English countryside is more appropriate than the lines to "The Ruinous Abbey" taken from his volume, *Winged Chariot and Other Poems:*

> Stilled the meek glory of thy music
>   Now only the wild linnets sing
> Along the confusion of thy ruins
>   And to cold echo sing.

> Quenched the wan purple of thy windows,
>   The light-thinned saffron and the red;
> Now only on the sword of thy dominion
>   Eve's glittering gold is shed.

> Oh, all the fair rites of thy religion!—
>   Gone now the pomp, the ashen grief;

Lily of Easter and wax of Christmas;
  Grey water, chrism, and sheaf!

Lift up thy relics to Orion;
  Display thy green attire to the sun;
Forgot thy tombs, forgot thy names and places;
  Thy peace forever won!

The undertone of de la Mare's irony in the peace that is found beyond names and places and the rites of religion is faint but clear; the very organ-like tones of the poem cover it, yet it is there, quite as, in an early poem, "Your ghost (is) where your face was." And, of course, the same watchful art pervades the poem, guides its music and selects the phrase.

No poet in elder age since Yeats has kept his art more watchful and alive than de la Mare has; and like Yeats, he has mastered his privilege to write in the full richness of the lyrical tradition of English verse, a privilege which leaves him free, with that freedom which comes only through the mastery of form, to draw upon the resources of memory, and with these resources, to speak in accents of authority and that few poets of the past or of our own century possess. It is improbable that a young poet, however gifted, could have written the following lines of "She Said" (in *Winged Chariot and Other Poems*):

She said, "I will come back again
  As soon as breaks the morn."
But the lark was wearying of the blue,
  The dew dry on the thorn,
  And all was still forlorn.

She said, "I will come back again,
  At the first quick stroke of noon."
But the birds were hid in the shade from the heat
  When the clock tolled, No: *but soon!*
  And then beat slowly on.

She said, "Yes, I'll be back again
  Before the sun has set."

But the sweetest promises often made
  Are the easiest to forget,
  No matter grief and fret . . .

That moon, now silvering in the east,
  One shadow casts—my own.
Thought I, my friend, how often we
Have shared this solitude. And see,
  Midnight will soon draw on,
When the last leaf of hope is fallen,
And silence haunts heart's vacancy,
And even pining's done.

The observation in this poem is drawn from memory and
the experience of time, and the metaphysics of time and space
have been among the recurrent themes of de la Mare's poetry.
It is consistent with the character of de la Mare's wit that it
should recall in the title of his long poem "Winged Chariot"
Andrew Marvell's lines "To His Coy Mistress," and without effort, a familiar association of time is presented to the
reader. Once that association with Marvell's lines is struck,
it is de la Mare's wit that guides the poem. It is easy enough
to say that the poem is neither narrative nor dramatic in design: it is rather, a meditative poem, a monologue on time,
which implies, through the most artful of disguises, the progress of a spiritual autobiography behind it. No one but de la
Mare could or would make a poem of this kind; and few
poets of this century would trust their technical skill to the
writing of a long poem in the rhymed *terza rima,* and this
with all possible variations upon that form. One can be
safe in saying that there is not a dull line in it, that the technical brilliance of the poem often threatens to outshine its
metaphysics and that it has the dangerous air of being a tour
de force. Like all of de la Mare's writing at its best it demands
more than a single reading; yet even in quotation some measure of its depth may be glimpsed in the following passage:

The very soul's at gaze, as if in trance:
Poised like a condor in the Andean night,
When scarp and snowdrift, height of pinnacled
 height,
Transmute with wonder the first morning
 light.

So, in its innocence, love breaks upon sight.

Hatred, dread, horror, too. As books relate:—
Thyestes when his own son's flesh he ate;
First stare at his iron cage of Bajazet;
And Oedipus—when parricide's his fate.

These lines have a variety and crispness that have been
achieved by few poets since Pope wrote his *Moral Essays* in
heroic couplets; and de la Mare's technical achievement is of
like quality:

So, out of morning mist earth's flowers arise,
Reflecting tintless daybreak in the skies;
And, soon, the whole calm orient with its dyes.

And even in bleak Winter one may go
Out of night's waking dreams and see the snow
In solemn glory on the fields below.

How happy he whose 'numbers' well as sweet,
Their rhythms in tacit concert with their feet,
And measure 'time,' with no less hushed a beat . . .

And clepsydra—the clock that Plato knew,
Tolling the varying hours each season through;
Oozing on, drop by drop, in liquid flow,
Its voice scarce audible, bell-like and low
As Juliet's communings with her Romeo.

More silent yet; pure solace to the sight—
The dwindling candle with her pensive light
Metes out the leaden watches of the night,
And, in that service, from herself takes flight.

I shall leave to other readers and critics the pleasure of finding the uses and ambiguities which de la Mare plays upon a favorite word like "sweet"; I shall leave to others the rediscovery of his felicity in choosing adjectives that seem as innocent as "tintless" and "pensive," and are so indisputably right in the way he places them. I am more concerned with the quality of wit which is revealed and is central to the character of his imagination in his last remark upon the candle: "And in that service, from herself takes flight." It is such lines as these that the particular, the peculiar quality of de la Mare's genius finds its expression; the same presence is felt in his *Memoirs of a Midget,* which has become a classic of its kind, and in the short story, "Miss Duveen"; it is an act of revelation, with the least possible commentary, ethical or otherwise, which concerns the nature of the world that he has seen, as if in a vision, for more than three quarters of a century. Undoubtedly, "Winged Chariot" is the best of de la Mare's longer poems, but it is also among the very few excellent long poems written in the twentieth century. Since, in a poem of this kind the full life of a poet's imaginative being is implied in the making of it, it has an authority that is not to be measured by its external brilliance nor the actual time spent in writing it. To other poets—and de la Mare is a poets' poet as well as one whose lyrics and narratives have caught and held the attention of the popular ear—his example reasserts the presence of magic in poetry which is commonly sought for and rarely found.

The Gothic Imagination
and the Survival of
Thomas Lovell Beddoes

IT WOULD BE EASY, AND I believe, several degrees too easy, to speak of Thomas Lovell Beddoes as a lesser Byron. At first glance, Byron and Beddoes seem fortunately linked: both were extraordinarily precocious, both enjoyed the freedom of living away from home in exile on the European continent, both found a release for creative energy in revolutionary politics, both were experienced in the writing of poetic drama, and both men welcomed death on foreign shores. But beyond this rough analogy the comparison begins to fail, and indeed it illustrates the not unfamiliar difficulty that has come into being by freely tossing the names of a half-dozen early nine-teenth-century British poets into undue proximity; in this confusion we find the poetry of Keats and Shelley bound between covers of a single volume, and the same darkness hovers over thoroughly respectable academic discussions of all figures grouped under the heading of "The Romantic Movement." It is all too seldom that true and pertinent distinctions are made within this convenient group of attractive names, for names in close company, like coins jingled too frequently together, lose their faces, and in literary discourse, many names are worn to faceless brilliance in the jargon of studious research and re-appreciation.

If the temptation exists to place Beddoes in biographical proximity to Byron, an even greater temptation to view him as a belated Elizabethan has not been resisted. If we could be content with a second glance at Beddoes' works in the huge, eight-hundred-page volume, so devotedly, almost devoutly edited by Dr. H. W. Donner,[1] we would agree with the reiterated opinions of Lytton Strachey, which were dutifully followed by Mr. F. L. Lucas, and George Saintsbury. All opinions chimed to the belated Elizabethan character of Beddoes' poetry—nor was the epithet entirely without foundation. Beddoes' literary indebtedness to Marlowe, Marston, Webster, and Tourneur was of no inconsiderable weight; he read them with the fascination and joy that Keats described at his discovering Chapman's Homer. In reading for ourselves the shadowed pages and the luminous passages of Beddoes' Gothic mystery play, *Death's Jest Book,* we are in little danger of forgetting the impress that Marlowe and Webster had left upon them—that is all too obvious, and to deny it would be as futile as denying Wordsworth's debt to Milton. Granting all this, the best of Beddoes' poetry merits a third reading, and in a final consideration a balance may be struck between a Victorian neglect of Beddoes' virtues and the excitement of their rediscovery in the twentieth century.

The story of Beddoes' extraordinary, brief, ineffectual, and obscure career has been told at length in Dr. Donner's definitive biography. Like many a patient, pure-minded labor of love, Dr. Donner's book[2] has earned respect, if not reciprocal enthusiasm, and its sheets have not been imported to the United States. Beddoes' personality was of the same psychic disorder and maladjustment that shaped the behavior of Rimbaud in the nineteenth century and Hart Crane in the

---

[1] *The Works of Thomas Lovell Beddoes,* edited with an introduction by H. W. Donner. London: Oxford University Press, 1935.

[2] *Thomas Lovell Beddoes: The Making of a Poet,* by H. W. Donner. Basil Blackwell: Oxford University Press, 1935.

twentieth, yet the environment of his early youth was far more fortunate than theirs; he was the son of the prosperous and notoriously eccentric Dr. Thomas Beddoes and a nephew of the witty and gifted Maria Edgeworth. At the age of nineteen and while still an undergraduate at Pembroke College, Oxford, he achieved celebrity through the publication of his play in verse, *The Bride's Tragedy*—and in the second year after Keats's death in 1823, Beddoes received more spontaneous and authoritative praise than any young poet of his generation. Two years later, he had left Pembroke for the University of Göttingen, leaving England, and his "ambition to become poetically distinguished" behind him. Yet, as his friend, Thomas Forbes Kelsall, knew, Beddoes had already started work on the dramatic poem, *Death's Jest Book,* which was to become the true object of his ambitions and to haunt his imagination for the next twenty years. Kelsall, and another friend, James Dykes Campbell, saw how persistently the growth of *Death's Jest Book* broke through and was nourished by Beddoes' studies in medicine, and they were also in a position to know, through correspondence, the restless, guilt-haunted temper of Beddoes' intelligence, its release of energy in political oratory at Würzburg, its violence, its ardors, and the reaches of its last expression at its deathbed, "I am food for *what I am good for*—worms."

But even death itself and probable suicide in 1849 (which Dr. Donner established as a near certainty) did not check the pursuit of Nemesis which shadowed Beddoes' frame. Beddoes' misplaced confidence in Bryan Waller Procter's (Barry Cornwall's) critical advice, which had smoothly glanced across the surfaces of fragmentary pieces from Beddoes' pen with an impartial lack of understanding, repeated its cycle in 1883 when Robert Browning, who had promised Kelsall that he would edit and publish Beddoes' manuscripts, called in the assistance of Sir Edmund Gosse. Both Sir Edmund and Browning were shocked at what they found within the box that Kelsall left them, and for the moment the incident served only to permit Dykes Campbell to make a transcript of everything the box contained. We shall never be quite clear as to exactly what horrified the sensibilities of Gosse, but we do know that the box and its contents were handed over to the care of Browning's son, and were, thereafter irrevocably lost. Gosse, with his adroit and habitual negligence, issued an edition of Beddoes' poetry in 1890, and in 1928 another edition appeared, prepared by Gosse and published in a manner that is usually reserved—including an evasive introduction and a garish typeface—for pornographia. Aside from a few scraps of actual manuscript, and a pamphlet of verse in German, what we read today in Dr. Donner's excellent edition of *The Works of Thomas Lovell Beddoes* are the copies made of Beddoes' poems in Dykes Campbell's hand.

Because of the ill-luck which attended the posthumous publication of Beddoes' poetry, it would seem that we approach it with the utmost difficulty. Sir Arthur Quiller-Couch's reprinting of a mutilated version of Beddoes' "Dream-Pedlary" in *The Oxford Book of English Verse* increased rather than diminished the general air of confusion which has so persuasively followed mention of Beddoes' name, and the question arises as to where and how the confusion originated. Were Procter, Browning, Gosse, and Sir Arthur wholly responsible for the obscurity of Beddoes' fame? It must be confessed that they materially aided its long career of darkness, but its true source lies in the uneasy relationship which existed between Beddoes and his work; self-knowledge was of slow and fatal growth within him, and when it came, it came too late. There was more of self-realization than of true humility or of pathos in Beddoes' last note to Revell Phillips: "I ought to have been among other things a good poet." It is not enough to say with Dr. Donner that Beddoes lacked self-confidence; the psychic split which marred his character and brought his private life within the area that we reserve for Rimbaud and

Hart Crane, ran deeper than any loss of confidence in what he wrote. The attitude that he adopted toward his poetry swung between and often touched the two extremes of desiring an absolute perfection in its expression and the impulse to destroy it utterly, yet the ambition to write voluminously, to be heard, to speak aloud remained. His miscalculation in measuring the quality of Procter's literary friendship could almost be described as an act of literary suicide; it was his sin against the mark of his own genius, which had left its impress upon every brilliant passage that comes to light in the tortured progress of writing *Death's Jest Book*.

Beyond the sources of literary stimulation which Beddoes received from a reading of the lesser Elizabethan dramatists, was his greater effort to clothe and vitalize the spirit and temper of the Gothic myth, the genius that had created the gargoyles on the towers of Notre Dame, the giantchild Gargantua, the merry voyages of Pantagruel, the fiery journey of Mad Meg across Flanders, the Dance of Death itself (which actually enters a scene of *Death's Jest Book*), the very genius that had found its revival in Matthias Claudius' brief and exquisite lyric, *Der Tod und das Mädchen*. Beddoes' prose version of death and the maiden appears in semi-classical disguise in "The Tale of the Lover to his Mistress":

> After the fall of Jupiter came Love one night to Psyche: it was dark in her cottage and she began to strike a light. "Have done," said he, in a low whispering tone—in which the hinge of some dreadful dark truth out of another world seemed to turn. "Youth, power, and heaven have passed away from the gods: the curse of age has changed their shapes:—then seek not to look on me, Psyche; but if thou art faithful, kiss me, and we will then go into the darkness for ever."— "How art thou changed?" asked she; "methinks you do but try me, jestingly, for thou canst only have grown more beautiful. That thou art more powerful I hear, for the night air is full of rushing arrows, and many are struck and sigh. Hast thou lost thy wings that were so glorious?"—"Aye, but I am swifter than of old."—"Thy youth?"— "Aye, but I am stronger: all must fall before me."—"Thy charms and

wiles?"—"Aye, but he whom I have once stricken, is mine for ever and ever."—"Why should I not see thee then? Art thou Love no more?"—"Aye, but not fleeting, earthly; eternal, heavenly Love."— Just then the moon rose, and Psyche saw beside her a gaunt anatomy, through which the blue o' th' sky shone and the stars twinkled, gold promises beaming through Death, armed with arrows, bearing an hour-glass. He stepped with her to the sea-side, and they sank where Venus rose.

The attraction that the Gothic imagination held for Beddoes may be sought well outside the boundaries of his great admiration for Webster, Marston, and Marlowe, and the forces that drew him toward it were as strong as the impulse which Coleridge felt in the writing of "The Rime of the Ancient Mariner":

> Are those her ribs through which the Sun
> Did peer as through a grate?
> And is that woman all her crew?
> Is that a Death? and are there two?
> Is Death that woman's mate?
>
> Her lips were red, her looks were free,
> Her locks were yellow as gold:
> Her skin was as white as leprosy,
> The Nightmare Life-in-Death was she,
> Who thicks man's blood with cold.

The genius toward which Beddoes moved was of an elder heritage and of the same, yet deeper root than any reading of the Elizabethan dramatists would disclose; the power of attraction had its true origins behind the façades of Renaissance literature at their noontide; Beddoes' effort to re-create a truly Gothic metaphysic from the slowly increasing manuscript of *Death's Jest Book* was, if anything, kept alive and nurtured by his residence on central European soil, and the impulse which lay behind the creation of his incompleted masterpiece was as clear a symptom of his day as Coleridge's "Ancient Mariner" or

Sir Walter Scott's translation of Goethe's remarkable *Erlkönig*. Truly enough *Death's Jest Book* restrung and hinged together the common properties of Renaissance poetic drama, and among them the network of double plots and motives inspired by revenge, but what is important for us to rediscover is Beddoes' persistent stress upon those elements in Webster and in Marlowe in which the sources ran backward to the Middle Ages; and there it was that Beddoes had made his choice. Like Edgar Poe, Beddoes was a late arrival on the Romantic scene, and like the American poet, his lyricism expressed a last if fragmentary refinement of a first phase in Romantic emotion that had traced its conscious origins to the *Lyrical Ballads* of 1798. His fantastically late resurrection has blurred, almost beyond recognition, his true position within the literature of his day. No echoes of his voice were heard within it beyond the strains of that eminently precocious venture, *The Bride's Tragedy;* and Procter's friendly indifference had closed the door to those in England who might have heard him with a reawakened ear.

Since I have viewed at length the unfortunate aspects of Beddoes' career and its subsequent miscarriages of fame, one should modify that unequitable balance by saying that Dr. Donner's edition of his *Works* appeared at a particularly happy moment for their twentieth-century revival. If Beddoes' relationship to his creative gifts and their fulfillment was, to put it mildly, sporadic and uncertain, their radical nature was remarkably consistent. In that respect alone, his life, his work, his political convictions, and the quality of his imagination resemble what we have read in the poems, the letters, and notebooks of Gerard Manley Hopkins. Because of the singular likeness in radical temper, it can be said with certain obvious reservations that the discovery of Hopkins' poems immediately following the first World War prepared the critics for a favorable reception of Dr. Donner's edition of Beddoes' *Works*. In the middle 1930's and on both sides of the Atlantic, writers of conservative beliefs as well as left, sought out their origins of a radical heritage, and in this sense the revival of Beddoes' name carried with it associations of particular significance; and Beddoes' participation in revolutionary activity was of a nature that paralleled the activity of young British writers in the Spanish Civil War.

Beddoes' career in Germany and Switzerland had been marked by the writing of political satires, and the most successful of these were written in his adopted German, a language which he spoke with rapidly increasing facility. They were done as though he were on holiday from his major work in *Death's Jest Book,* as though the shift in language were a release from the demands of seeking the perfected line, the absolute phrase, the final word. Quite as *The Bride's Tragedy* had achieved distinction as a tour de force in the revival of Elizabethan dramatic verse, Beddoes' brilliantly turned political satires served a lively purpose in expressing the radical spirit of his time; among these, there are speeches and verses which were in effect a triple-edged attack on the forces that sanctioned the Holy Alliance, the Church itself, and reactionary German poetry. Quickened by Beddoes' wit and energy the German language was transformed into parody of itself, and what Beddoes had learned from reading Rabelais came to light in his pamphlet which contained verses "On the Enemies of David Friedrich Strauss," his *Antistraussianischer Gruss.* To find their equal one must turn to John Skelton's satire *Why Come Ye Not to Court* or to certain passages of James Joyce's *Finnegans Wake;* and it is also of historical interest to remember that David Strauss and the incident which inspired the verse left an impression on the early education of Karl Marx. The pamphlet found an appreciative audience among Swiss and German revolutionaries, and its distribution warned educational authorities in central Europe of a certain medical student, Herr Beddoes, a little Englishman, who on one occasion at least had roused fellow students to revolt by reciting a mock tribute to the dying Wellington, "Prussia's one Field Marshal."

How deeply these activities affected the revised versions of *Death's Jest Book,* we shall never know, but in the play of plot and counterplot in Beddoes' Gothic melodrama, the forces of established power, of revolution, and of counterrevolution run their bloody courses, motivated by revenge. The two Fools in the play (and originally it was subtitled, *The Fool's Tragedy*) seem to speak in Beddoes' voice and certainly they recite a number of his finest lyrics, but what of Mario, a character who seeks a leader and who speaks with memorable eloquence?

> A Roman am I;
> A Roman in unroman times: I've slept
> At midnight in our Capitolian ruins,
> And breathed the ghost of our great ancient world,
> Which there doth walk: and among glorious visions,
> That the unquiet tomb sent forth to me,
> Learned I the love of Freedom. Scipio saw I
> Washing the stains of Carthage from his sword,
> And his freed poet, playing on his lyre
> A melody men's souls replied unto:
> Oak-bound and laurelled heads, each man a country;
> And in the midst, like a sun o'er the sea
> (Each helm in the crowd gilt by a ray from him),
> Bald Julius sitting lonely in his car,
> Within the circle of whose laurel wreath
> All spirits of the earth and sea were spell-bound.
> Down with him to the grave! Down with the god!
> Stab, Cassius; Brutus, through him; through him, all!
> Dead.—As he fell there was a tearing sigh:
> Earth stood on him; her roots were in his heart;
> They fell together. Caesar and his world
> Lie in the Capitol; and Jove lies there,
> With all the gods of Rome and of Olympus; . . .

Despite the weight of inversions in Mario's speech, despite the rhetorical extravagance of "Down with him to the grave!

Down with the god!" which show the marks of Schiller's influence as well as the intonations of a distinctly unmodulated school of German acting, the speech reveals a clear and vivid strength of movement that distinguishes the best of Beddoes' poetry from the work of his better known contemporaries. The historical imagination which finds its voice within the speech displays an insight of remarkable force and energy, and is of that quality which we associate with the utterance of prophetic truth.

Perhaps *Death's Jest Book* by the very weight of its intentions was foredoomed to remain imperfect and unfinished; perhaps there is prophetic significance in the shift of its subtitle from *The Fool's Tragedy* to *The Day Will Come,* that is, the day of its completion placed forever in the future. Quite as D. H. Lawrence was never to complete the larger plan of *The Rainbow,* or as Keats *Hyperion* remains a fragment, or as Hart Crane's *The Bridge* could not attain the elaborated structure of its early inspiration, so *Death's Jest Book* falls short of its original design. The desire to create a work of all-embracing stature and dimensions is one of the deepest and most frequently noted pitfalls of the Romantic imagination; surely its shadows haunted Coleridge's "Kubla Khan" and his ode, "Dejection," and from then onward the path went downward into the darkness of being unable to write poetry at all. The last days of Beddoes' life were spent in the same darkness, yet before his work can be dismissed as one who "had made failure his vocation," some attention must be given to two short poems, which are, to my knowledge, among the best examples of lyric verse written in Beddoes' generation.

Since the complete version of "Dream-Pedlary" still lacks the public it deserves, and since the quality of its imagination merits its rediscovery in all discussions of nineteenth-century poetry, I need not apologize for including an entire quotation of it here:

I

If there were dreams to sell,
  What would you buy?
Some cost a passing bell;
  Some a light sigh,
That shakes from Life's fresh crown
Only a roseleaf down.
If there were dreams to sell,
Merry and sad to tell,
And the crier rung the bell,
  What would you buy?

II

A cottage lone and still,
  With bowers nigh,
Shadowy, my woes to still,
  Until I die.
Such pearl from Life's fresh crown
Fain would I shake me down.
Were dreams to have at will,
This would best heal my ill,
  This would I buy.

III

But there were dreams to sell,
  Ill didst thou buy;
Life is a dream, they tell,
  Waking, to die.
Dreaming a dream to prize,
Is wishing ghosts to rise;
  And, if I had the spell
  To call the buried, well,
    Which one would I?

IV

If there are ghosts to raise,
  What shall I call,
Out of hell's murky haze,
  Heaven's blue hall?
Raise my loved longlost boy
To lead me to his joy.
  There are no ghosts to raise;
  Out of death lead no ways;
    Vain is the call.

V

Know'st thou not ghosts to sue?
  No love thou hast.
Else lie, as I will do,
  And breathe thy last.
So out of Life's fresh crown
Fall like a roseleaf down.
   Thus are the ghosts to woo;
   Thus are all dreams made true,
    Ever to last!

Not even the sensitively gifted Tennyson of *The Lady of Shalott* or of the lyrical interludes in "Maud" quite equals the play of sound and echo, of sight and recall of image that weave and finally complete the garland so gracefully thrown across death's shoulders in "Dream-Pedlary." One would probably have a better chance of finding an equal among Hölderlin's lyrical remains, rather than in any selection of English poetry, but even there, only the like quality of spirit may be sought and not the melodic variations of Beddoes' lines. In contemporary poetry, the nearest approach to Beddoes' lyric imagery may be found in the following lines from Walter de la Mare; the spirit has thinned and grown remote, but its shadow lingers:

Not toward Death, who, stranger, fairer,
Than any siren turns his head—
Than sea-couched siren, arched with rainbows,
Where knell the waves of her ocean bed.
Alas, that beauty hangs her flowers
For lure of his demoniac powers:
Alas, that from these eyes should dart
Such piercing summons to thy heart;
That mine in frenzy of longing beats,
Still lusting for these gross deceits.
    Not that way!

As one reads through the prose and verse fragments of *The Ivory Gate,* supposedly written by Beddoes between the years

1833 to 1838, the likeness of his verse and its imagery turns in the direction of his distant, and almost certainly unknown to him, American contemporary, Edgar Poe; unfinished manuscripts bearing the title, "The City of the Sea" appear, and the best (and apparently completed) union of prose and verse among the scattered papers is "Thanatos to Kenelm":

"I have no feeling for the monuments of human labour," she would say, "the wood and the desert are more peopled with my household gods than the city or the cultivated country. Even with the living animals and the prevailing vegetation of the forest in this hemisphere, I have little sympathy. I know not the meaning of a daisy, nor what nature has symbolized by the light bird and the butterfly. But the sight of a palm with its lofty stem and tuft of long grassy leaves, high in the blue air, or even such a branch as this (breaking off a large fern leaf) awake in me a feeling, a sort of nostalgy and longing for ages long past. When my ancient sire used to sit with me under the old dragon tree or Dracaena, I was as happy as the ephemeral fly balanced on his wing in the sun, whose setting will be his death-warrant. But why do I speak to you so? You cannot understand me."—And then she would sing whisperingly to herself:

> The mighty thoughts of an old world
> Fan, like a dragon's wing unfurled,
>   The surface of my yearnings deep;
> And solemn shadows then awake,
> Like the fish-lizard in the lake,
>   Troubling a planet's morning sleep.
>
> My waking is a Titan's dream,
> Where a strange sun, long set, doth beam
>   Through Montezuma's cypress bough:
> Through the fern wilderness forlorn
> Glisten the giant hart's great horn
>   And serpents vast with helmed brow.
>
> The measureless from caverns rise
> With steps of earthquake, thunderous cries,
>   And graze upon the lofty wood;

> The palmy grove, through which doth gleam
> Such antediluvian ocean's stream,
>   Haunts shadowy my domestic mood.

It is highly probable that the speech and its song were originally spoken by Sibylla, one of the heroines of *Death's Jest Book,* that the song appeared in an early draft of the play's first act, and was later discarded from the revised versions. Like many passages within the play, the speech and the song circumscribe a completed unit of emotion and the forms which embody it, and as such it is one of the purest expressions of the Romantic genius in ninetenth-century literature. The first line of the song's last stanza recalls, of course, Coleridge's famous "caverns measureless to man," but on reading the entire passage, the impulse is to remark how Poesque it is, how gently it enters and then deeply penetrates the world that lives behind the conscious mind and eye; there it discloses as the song is sung the center of the world so persistently sought by the Romantic imagination, the heart of reality within the dream.

Beddoes' characteristic imagery in the song, its dragon's wing and its fish-lizard were of the world as Pythagoras saw it, and did not anticipate, as Dr. Donner justly observes, the themes of nineteenth-century evolution. But Beddoes' visual imagery has still another field of association and in that field strikes deeply at the roots of a mythology which has its being in continental Europe; his Satanism whenever it appears takes on the character of Pieter Brueghel's canvases; and in reading the lyrical interludes of *Death's Jest Book,* one carries the images of Brueghel's "The Triumph of Death" and "The Fall of the Rebel Angels" before the eye—and it is that aspect of reality which is perceived and brought to life beneath the surface of the modern world.

Beddoes' power to reawaken the images of Gothic heritage has its own force today; and in Poe's words, the death that looks gigantically down, stares with peculiar intensity upon the map of twentieth-century Europe. Covered with the pall of re-armored warfare, one may perceive in the center of that map, the diminished figure of Beddoes' great Fool, Mandrake, and if one listens one may hear a few lines from a stanza of his song; the scene is lit only by flares dropped from the sky; death's triumph lingers there through broken streets and hallways, and human terror resumes its mask of Gothic irony:

> Folly hath now turned out of door
> Mankind and Fate, who were before
> Jove's Harlequin and Clown.
> The world's no stage, no tavern more,
> Its sign, the Fool's ta'en down.

Samuel Johnson
in the
Twentieth Century

As ONE TURNS THE PAGES of Samuel Johnson's *Poems,* many questions are opened to the mind, and the first of these is a test of our general interest in the eighteenth century. Why is Johnson's verse read today, and why is it that both his verse and prose awaken respect as well as curiosity? Two generations ago quotations from Boswell's *Life of Johnson* occasioned more amusement than enjoyment or a serious regard, and the occasion (inspired perhaps by readings of Macaulay, Thackeray, and Taine) was a signal for hilarity rather than respect. But to continue with our question: Is the revival of Johnson a mere turning of the wheel that raises the fame of one writer and his age and obscures the others, a recurrent movement accompanied by the cries of "Down with Shelley, up with Pope; it is growing far too late for Donne and Crashaw, therefore, up with Johnson—and do not forget that excellent though neglected poet, Christopher Smart"? Is our interest in Johnson's major writings, his lives of Milton, Savage, and Pope, *The Vanity of Human Wishes* and his *London* a subconscious desire to unsay Wordsworth's *Preface* to the second edition of the *Lyrical Ballads?*—that preface which was written in the wraithlike but resounding presence of Johnson's authority and which dispelled it for a hundred years to come? I think not. Nor is our general curiosity concerning an age that was devout, and yet followed the lights of reason, a complete rejection of all nineteenth-century notions of progress in the worship of scientific skills and innovations. This general question, no matter how briefly answered, and in which I may have seemed to persist at length, supplies a key and perhaps unlocks a door to a few of the multiple reasons why Johnson's stature has not decreased during a generation that has felt the earth shake with the impact of two World Wars. In times such as our own, the best of serious writing reflects the strength of radical convictions (and Johnson was decidedly radical in his expression of conservative beliefs), all scenes that mirror that origin of our institutions as they are today attain the power and vividness of a renewed perception into the heart of human activity. In England—and I am thinking of the island and not the near and far reaches of the British Empire—the appeal of an eighteenth-century formality in literary diction, wit, and manner has its own elegiac, and one might say, "romantic" air. It is the same heightened mood that a young man or woman achieves in a last look about the house before leaving home for foreign lands; the look embraces all things with an unconscious lift of being: chairs, tables, doors, and windows take on the quality of animate life and seem to speak; and for the first time, each in its proper place acquires meanings that hitherto had been left in darkness, and until this moment had been unfelt, unknown. Something of that sensibility, which one hesitates to call "emotion," has been conveyed by Edith Sitwell's book on Bath and in her *Alexander Pope;* and one finds that in her literary essays Virginia Woolf is at her happiest when she brings to mind Dr. Burney's evening parties in Poland Street, or the masks that Horace Walpole wore to face the world. These are tributes written to a past which has an imaginative being within the present, but is perceived in the twentieth century as though it were seen for the last time. On our side of the Atlantic the memory of eighteenth-century imagination revives the day that saw the birth of our governmental institutions; and remembering them, we accept the contradictions of our early national heroes, Washington, Adams, Hamilton, Marshall, and Jefferson, as a peculiarly American complex whose continuity remains unbroken and today reasserts its claim to an enduring life.

We can then agree, I think, that with all the visible changes which have taken place in the last two hundred years, differences in dress, in architecture, in social habits, in modes of speech and of travel, our general outlook toward the eighteenth century is neither disinterested, nor unreasonably cold. But in speaking of so broad a view and looking into a new edition of Johnson's *Poems,* another question rises: What of Johnson's view, how far did it go, was it clear or clouded; did it run farther than that queer distance he described "from China to Peru," by air or land or sea, and did it in a final glance embrace the world? That is a pertinent question in a day when world views are extremely popular and the names of many places ring in our ears. We wait for news from foreign correspondents, we rely on photographs of distant towns and cities, and some of us have perfected the means of tuning in casually on television; the view is globular and swift, but not, I fear, completely translatable to sight and feeling on the written page. In articles and even in books of considerable bulk written by experts, so I have heard, of world affairs, the *Weltanschauung* grows thin with the blue of empyrean distances: whole nations, plateaus, valleys, mountain ranges, and even continents are bombed off the earth, replanned, and perhaps repopulated within a single paragraph; the world view, since we must have it, is still there, but its skirts (if I may change the figure) are of sheerest organdy, and the lady looks shameless, anemic, and about to perish in a winter storm. A world view of this sort, I must confess, does not appear in Johnson's prose or verse, nor does a world view of another kind, and of a sort expressed by the deliberate philosopher: a Thomas Hobbes, a Bishop Berkeley, or a Professor Whitehead, enter the central stream of Johnson's morality. Despite the strength of Johnson's will and mind, it would be possible to argue that he was not an intellectual at all, and if we insist upon reading a world view into the content of Johnson's verse we must speak in terms of a theology nourished by the Anglican Church, and then agree that it was a different order than that which possessed the imagination of his peers.

It is of some significance to know that in conversation Johnson's vowels were spoken with the same accent which marked the speech of his fellow countrymen at Lichfield, and that many years of living in the city of London could not alter them. David Garrick, mimicking his old schoolmaster's voice, rolling head and heaving shoulders, once shouted, "Who's for the *poonsh?*" to the great joy of the assembled company. One need not labor the point that Johnson was firmly of his time and place, and more than that, was at least two decades behind the moment at which his influence was most deeply felt. If it can be said that one drop of provincialism in a man's blood makes all mankind his kin, then Johnson's heavy frame and swelling veins contained a full pint of that heady liquor. At the moment of his celebrity in London he moved as an ancient Titan in the company of a highly self-conscious and sophisticated group of young and active men; he was the father of their "Literary Club," voicing taboos and parental discriminations among its members; his corpulent figure was the totem of their belief, and his contrasting fits of kindness, or anger, or of despair were the signs of his all-too-human relationship to earth. He entered the latter and declining years of the Augustan Age with the conventions of Queen Anne's day unflawed, untarnished: from the sources of Juvenal, Horace, Dryden, and Pope he drew sustenance for the external forms of his literary style, and it should be added that however well he knew his Greek, his skills were Latin, corresponding to the usefulness, the spans, and masses of the Roman aqueduct. But the melancholy strains within the forms, transfiguring the style and making it his own, were not of the European continent nor of its southern peninsulas:

> Year chases year, decay pursues decay,
> Still drops some joy from with'ring life away.

These strains are of a northern heritage, sounded in the epic of *Beowulf* and heard within the soliloquies of *Hamlet* and *Macbeth,* and their last echoes are resumed beyond Johnson's century in the dramatic verse of Henrik Ibsen. Perhaps it could be said that something which resembles or runs parallel to a *Weltanschauung* has been conveyed within the measures that define the melancholy temper, but we can say that all poetry worthy of our admiration enjoys a happy paradox of seeming most universal when it is most at home, voiced in a language that intones a familiar tongue and is sheltered by the protection of its own rooftree. In this sense Johnson's major verse as it is represented by *The Vanity of Human Wishes* has elements of greatness that place it within comparable reaches of Gray's "Elegy in a Country Churchyard" and Wordsworth's "Resolutions and Independence." It was Johnson's profound look into the passions of life beyond the memories of youth that endowed his *Human Wishes* with a somber heat, and this perception is that of a writer who possesses "a tragic sense of life."

Of Johnson the moralist—and his morality was of the same root from which his melancholy sprang—it can be said that one finds him less oppressive and certainly less static than he seemed a generation or two ago. His texts for sermons, for the language that he wrote closely resembled the idiom of the pulpit in his day, were drawn from lively observations of the scene around him, a habit which he may have learned from an attentive reading of Dryden and Juvenal, but which, I think,

owes a slighter debt to literary influence than to the enforced
leisure of his unconquered indolence, to his love of walking
through crowded city streets, to his need for company in coffee-
houses and to the slow growth of his own literary fame. As
indolence increased his sense of guilt, the more urgent was his
demand to break its spell, and in that conflict his will was often
put to a test of strength between the prospect of lonely hours
at his desk or an evening's talk over several bottles of wine. His
imitation of Juvenal's *Third Satire*, his *London*, the verses of
which Pope had praised and predicted future celebrity for
their author, was constantly refreshed and kept in motion by
commentary that sharply reflected the diversions of life at the
nation's capital. The poem's wealth of contemporary reference
was so complete, so vivid in its detail that it has been all too
easy for studious readers of it to repeat and to half-accept Sir
John Hawkins' claim that "injur'd THALES," who "bids the
town farewell," was in fact a portrait of Johnson's old friend,
Richard Savage. For Thales, as we all know, was a wandering
Greek philosopher of the seventh century B.C., who left no
writings for posterity. It was he who believed that the single
imperishable element of worldly life was water, and the THALES
of the poem awaits a boat to take him out to sea; the classical
reference ignites the wit that follows after, and we who read
the poem today had better forget Sir John's attempt at scholarship and take our stand with Boswell who cheerfully denied
THALES' identity with Savage, and who knew his Johnson literally like a book.

In reading Johnson's moral verses we must grant that the
very terms of his theology have a further reach toward Heaven
and a greater depth than any Thales-like spread through flux
and motion; and in reading Johnson generally we should be
aware of the penetration, the delicate niceties with which he
viewed the weaknesses and merits of his fellow men. The
motives behind his observations were avowedly critical, but
the results as they appear in his verse and prose place Johnson

among the more profound psychologists of his age. The moralist who shouted warnings in Mrs. Thrale's drawing-room, and in one instance replied to her nephew's question as to whether or not the young man should marry by saying, "I would advise no man to marry, sir, who is not likely to prop-agate understanding," was at the very least a lexicographer well-schooled in the flaws of human character. The young man happened to be Sir John Lade, and Johnson afterward com-memorated the occasion of his asking an unfortunate question by writing the famous lines of "A Short Song of Congratula-tion" which appear in Sir Arthur Quiller-Couch's *Oxford Book of English Verse* under the less ironic title of "One-and-Twenty." But the fine balance with which Johnson weighed and sustained his judgments of human flaws and virtues was never better exemplified than in the concluding paragraphs of his *Life of Richard Savage*. The sermon was graced by an extraordinary, vital text, and I think I may be pardoned for quoting this particular passage at length, for the delicacy with which Johnson set his scales cannot be shown by citing isolated phrases:

He appeared to think himself born to be supported by others, and dispensed from all necessity of providing for himself; he therefore never prosecuted any scheme of advantage, nor endeavored even to secure the profits which his writings might have afforded him. His temper was, in consequence of the dominion of his passions, un-certain and capricious; he was easily engaged and easily disgusted; but he is accused of retaining his hatred more tenaciously than his benevolence.

He was compassionate by nature and principle, and was always ready to perform offices of humanity; but when he was provoked (and very small offenses were sufficient to provoke him) he would prosecute his revenge with the utmost acrimony till his passion had subsided.

His friendship was therefore of little value; for though he was zeal-ous in the support or vindication of those whom he loved, yet it was always dangerous to trust him, because he considered himself as discharged by the first quarrel from all ties of honor and gratitude, and would betray those secrets which in the warmth of confidence had been imparted to him. This practice drew upon him an universal accusation of ingratitude; nor can it be denied that he was very ready to set himself free from the load of an obligation; for he could not bear to convince himself in a state of dependence, his pride being equally powerful with his other passions, and appearing in the form of insolence at one time and of vanity at another. Vanity, the most innocent species of pride, was most frequently predominant: he could not easily leave off when he had once begun to mention himself or his works; nor even to read his verses without stealing his eyes from the page, to discover in the faces of the audience how they were affected with any favorite passage.

It is here that we recognize in Richard Savage the character of men who are alive today; the individual and the type have by no means vanished from the earth, and we know them with the same familiarity that we rediscover Iago, Uncle Toby, Emma Bovary, or Cousin Pons among the faces of our contemporaries. In *Richard Savage* Johnson revealed the springs of human failure, and his creation walks upon a stage where curtains part and footlights gleam beyond the moment of a merely literary being.

Since we are on the subject of Johnson's *Lives of the Poets,* the occasion presents itself for a glance, however brief, at his generally underrated essay on Swift. It is true that Johnson's attitude toward Swift could not be described in terms of unprejudiced affection, for the difference in temperament between the celebrated lexicographer and the late dean of St. Patrick's would scarcely permit the semblance of a natural rapport. The character of Swift's education whose actual progress took place in Sir William Temple's library was of a seventeenth-century order, and in contrast to his tastes and discriminations, the literary preferences of both Pope and Johnson represented the learning of a new generation in English letters. If Johnson leaned backward in time to the conventions of Queen Anne's day, their limitations were fixed by the new order of an Augustan Age which took pride in acknowledging Dryden as its predecessor. The true gulf between Swift and Pope was of a far greater span than Swift's admiration of Pope's genius indicated, so great indeed that an appreciation of the gifts of one is almost certain to obscure the other's. An intelligent comparison of Swift's "Verses on the Death of Dr. Swift" with Pope's "Epistle to Dr. Arbuthnot" is a near impossibility, and the contrast is all the more obvious because the two poems bear a superficial likeness to each other; both delight the reader by a display of self-knowledge beyond all ordinary wit, yet the moment that delight is gratified, the distinctly separate merits of the two poems assert their individuality; as Swift moves backward to Butler's *Hudibras* and ultimately to the rough pleasantries of Skelton, Pope moves forward from Dryden to anticipate the sensibility of William Collins, and from this point onward all comparison becomes irrelevant. Another illustration of the impassable gulf between the imaginations of Pope and Swift is shown in verse written from a common source of literary inspiration. Both poets had read Ovid with unusual insight, but it is significant that Pope chose *The Heroides* on which to model his *Eloïsa to Abelard,* while Swift turned to the *Metamorphoses* for the inspiration of his "Baucis and Philemon." In his "Baucis" Swift ran closer to the effects produced by the graphic art of Hieronymus Bosch, and incidentally to the twentieth century of Max Ernst and Yves Tanguy than to the world of Pope's *Eloïsa* and his "Elegy to the Memory of an Unfortunate Lady." A quotation from the transformation scene in "Baucis" clearly shows the trend of Swift's direction:

> The Groaning Chair began to crawl
> Like an huge Snail along the Wall;
> There stuck aloft, in Publick View,
> And with small Change, a Pulpit grew.

> The Porringers, that in a Row
> Hung high and made a glit'ring Show,
> To a less Noble Substance chang'd,
> Were now but Leathern Buckets rang'd.
>
> The Ballads pasted on the Wall
> Of *Joan of France,* and *English Moll,*
> *Fair Rosamond,* and *Robin Hood,*
> The *Little Children in the Wood:*
> Now seemed to look abundance better,
> Improv'd in Picture, Size, and Letter;
> And high in Order plac'd describe
> The Heraldry of ev'ry Tribe.
>
> A Bedstead of the Antique Mode,
> Compact of Timber many a Load,
> Such as our Ancestors did use,
> Was Metamorphos'd into Pews;
> Which still their ancient Nature keep;
> By lodging Folks dispos'd to sleep.
>
> The Cottage by such Feats as these,
> Grown to a Church by just Degrees,
> The Hermits then desir'd their Host
> To ask for what he fancy'd most:
> *Philemon,* having paus'd a while,
> Return'd them Thanks in Homely Stile;
> Then said; my House is grown so Fine,
> Methinks, I still wou'd call it mine:
> I'm Old, and fain wou'd live at Ease,
> Make me the Parson, if you please.

I can think of no further reach away from the scene of magic which took place in Philemon's cottage than the following lines from *Eloïsa to Abelard,* which are as distant, let us say, as the sight of earth from Eloïsa's Heaven:

> Grace shines around her with serenest beams,
> And whisp'ring angels prompt her golden dreams.
> For her th' unfading rose of Eden blooms,
> And wings of seraphs shed divine perfumes;

For her the spouse prepares the bridal ring;
For her white virgins hymeneals sing;
To sounds of heavenly harps she dies away,
And melts in visions of eternal day.

It is plain enough (as I have more than hinted in the contrasts of Swift's verse with Pope's) that the *Life* of Swift reflects the same cast of mind which steered Johnson's hand as he wrote his famous remarks on the metaphysical poets of the seventeenth century, but the essay, more than all else, is refined and tempered by the need to present the case of Swift with decent clarity and justice; it would be difficult to unsay Johnson's tributes to Swift's originality, or to quarrel with his apt and highly complimentary report of Swift's character from the confidences of Dr. Delany to Lord Orrery. The point is that even here where Johnson's heart was not warmed by his subject, his scale of values was as delicately set as in his *Life of Richard Savage,* and from that balance we find a definition of Swift's style which has not been improved upon since the day that it was written:

> His delight was in simplicity. That he has in his works no metaphor, as has been said, is not true; but his few metaphors seem to be received rather by necessity than choice. . . . His sentences are never too much dilated or contracted; and it will not be easy to find any embarrassment in the complication of his clauses, any inconsequence in his connections, or abruptness in his transitions.

But Johnson's moral instrument, however finely tempered it came to be, was uncommonly slow in taking its proper shape, and surely in the writing of his own verse, Johnson cannot be credited with the brilliance nor accused of the sins of an unlearned precocity. His mistaken venture into poetic drama, his *Irene,* was an early work over which he labored intermittently for ten years. Its production by David Garrick at the Theatre Royal in 1749 crowned its failure. The story of the play is told at length, in Richard Knolles's *The Generall Historie of the Turkes* from which Johnson received his inspiration, his plot, and the not unseductive figure of his heroine, the beautiful Greek captive, Irene, who had become chief concubine in the household of Sultan Mahomet II. The Sultan's sacrifice of, his murder in fact, of Irene—to appease the critics of his inactivity in war—was neither a happy subject for Johnson's speculations on moral conduct nor was it convincing proof of his heroine's virtues. Nor were Johnson's abilities as a dramatic poet of sufficient energy to convert his lengthy and (it must be admitted) awkward phrasing of moral dialogues into scenes of action. His fortunate choice of epithet in writing verse was of a late maturity and one finds its best examples in the poems written some thirty-odd years after the evening which made public Irene's disaster in Drury Lane.

We reread Johnson for his last words rather than his first; and among them his *Irene* and *The Vanity of Human Wishes,* which were presented to public view in the same year, may be looked upon today as signs of a turning point in his literary development. The melancholy strains so distinctly overheard throughout the measures of *The Vanity of Human Wishes* continue their progress in the themes of his shorter poems. As Johnson passed the meridian of middle age, his temperament was emphatically less humanitarian than it was humane, and in this distinction we rediscover the high values that he found in masculine courage, individual integrity, and a devotion to the Christian faith. In his later verse it can be said that he practiced what he preached, and indeed the writing of his verse seemed to improve as the slowly growing volume of his prose enlarged from the *Life of Richard Savage* in 1744, through *Rasselas* in 1759, to the *Lives of the Poets* in 1779. Even if we remained unaided by Boswell's biography, the course of Johnson's mature development in verse could be traced in parallel lines to the greater exercise of his critical gifts in prose. It would seem that the authority of one proceeds from the other, until at last we are rewarded by "A Short Song of Congratulation" and his verses "On the Death of Dr. Robert Levet."

Today we reread them in a friendly spirit, for since the passage of the last two decades, even the unwary reader of verse is considerably less frightened by the presence of a critical attitude as it reveals itself in poetry; and I would say that the discovery of moral aphorisms concealed in verse is far less distressing today than it was before the arrival of poetry written by—to name three dissimilar poets—Thomas Hardy, E. A. Robinson, and T. S. Eliot. Despite Johnson's positive mistrust of metaphysical poets, the revival of their work which caused voluble excitement in literary circles twenty-five years ago, actually paved the road for a renewed awareness of his own merits. The step between a poetry that admits the existence of metaphysical realities and the poetry that expresses the need for religious devotion has always been a short one: in both the presence of a matured poetic intelligence is often happily fused with the creative heat of poetic imagination. It is that intelligence which we rediscover in the following stanzas from Johnson's elegy on Dr. Levet, and in finding it, we are led to appreciate its manly attitudes of religious devotion as well as its sensibility which links the moment of its composition to the poetic imagination of our own day:

> Well tried through many a varying year,
> See Levet to the grave descend;
> Officious, innocent, sincere,
> Of ev'ry friendless name the friend.
>
> .   .   .   .   .
>
> When fainting nature call'd for aid,
> And hov'ring death prepar'd the blow,
> His vig'rous remedy display'd
> The power of art without the show.
>
> .   .   .   .   .
>
> His virtues walk'd their narrow round,
> Nor made a pause, nor left a void;

>   And sure th' Eternal Master found
>   The single talent well employ'd.

After reading these lines it is not too much to say that the profound depth of Johnson's piety found its most felicitous expression in a last tribute to the friend who once shared his apartments in Bolt Court—the chaste, industrious, and almost anonymous London physician whose round of practice remained among the poor and was circumscribed by poverty.

Of the many adaptations from Horace that Johnson wrote, none has greater claim to merit than the one which is said to have been written within the last month of his life, on the sixteenth of November, 1784; and since Johnson's imitations of Horace are not generally known, it seems appropriate to make a full quotation of it here. The fifteenth and sixteenth lines as well as the last two couplets are among the best examples of imitation from the Latin that the eighteenth century has produced, and these were written in an age that regarded Horace as its master and imitation of his work as a fine art:

>   The snow dissolv'd no more is seen,
>   The fields, and woods, behold, are green,
>   The changing year renews the plain,
>   The rivers know their banks again,
>   The spritely Nymph and naked Grace
>   The mazy dance together trace.
>   The changing year's successive plan
>   Proclaims mortality to Man.
>   Rough Winter's blasts to Spring give way,
>   Spring yields to Summer's sovereign ray,
>   Then Summer sinks in Autumn's reign,
>   And Winter chills the World again.
>   Her losses soon the Moon supplies,
>   But wretched Man, when once he lies
>   Where Priam and his sons are laid,
>   Is naught but Ashes and a Shade.
>   Who knows of Jove who counts our score
>   Will toss us in a morning more?

What with your friend you nobly share
At least you rescue from your heir.
Not you, Torquatus, boast of Rome,
When Minos once has fix'd your doom,
Or Eloquence, or splendid birth,
Or virtue shall replace on earth.
Hippolytus unjustly slain
Diana calls to life in vain,
Nor can the might of Theseus rend
The chains of hell that hold his friend.

To read the verse of Johnson's declining years is to hear the voice of a singularly compact and unified literary personality, and I need not, I hope, insist that even in a literature and language which carry within them many diverse figures of a vital and enduring individuality, the phenomenon of a Samuel Johnson is extremely rare. Few writers have achieved his "integration of personality" (the phrase belongs to Dr. C. G. Jung, but my figure remains the corpulent lexicographer who received an honorary LL.D. from Oxford); and that state of being is perhaps the most frequently cherished hope of the individual of the present age. In England of the eighteenth century Johnson shared with Fielding and Smollet and even Laurence Sterne the will and authority, the patriarchal strength and tenderness of a wholly masculine genius that has not made its reappearance in British literature of the first order since the death of Thomas Hardy. The vigor of an indigenous wit that Boswell heard when Johnson remarked, "The Irish are a FAIR people, they never speak well of one another," has no voice among living Englishmen today. We can be assured that the voice is not forgotten among a people who have outfaced the terrors of total war and uncertain peace.

H. G. Wells:
A Wreath for the
Liberal Tradition

1

SEVERAL YEARS AGO I INVITED a British poet out to lunch. I
chose an Armenian restaurant in the upper twenties on Lex-
ington Avenue, that section of New York where behind half-
curtained windows one can almost fancy a return to the Soho
in London of twenty-five years ago. Certainly the atmosphere
was of other times, other places than the moment and place
where we found our seats, and of a slightly foreign air. The
setting was contagious; we were in a stage-set of somewhere
else. The poet's Bloomsbury accent—and he was among the
best talkers in London—became more pronounced as the conversation lost its bearings; he was always more persuasive than
ultimately convincing, and with a half-glitter from his fine
blue eyes—the conversation must be saved—he broke out
suddenly with: "Why doesn't someone write something about
H. G. Wells?" The question came out of the air and was un-
answered by either of us.

I might have said, but didn't, that it is difficult to place Wells
anywhere; he can't be put in a corner; he doesn't stay in the
nineteenth century where he belongs; he was never a poet or
an artist, yet he haunts our feelings and certain sections of our

minds. If today he happens to be a ghost in London, he is strangely more alive than the papers where so much of his journalism appeared. Though in his last years his journalism wore his mind thin, he had dearly loved it; after writing "outlines" of history, he continued to write from week to week, "outlines" of world affairs, "outlines" of the universe, and his conclusions, even in the thinnest of his prose, were always more often right than wrong. His friends reported that shortly before his death during the midsummer of 1946 he had grown weary, but he had spoken of fatigue twelve years earlier, and wrote his *Experiment in Autobiography* in anticipation of death; the book gave him as he wrote it, "freedom of mind"; that was what he wanted before death, and he could afford to take it, in a house whose windows looked out over Regent's Park.

Wells was born in 1866. The time and place was Dickens' England and Wells was born into the same social strata where Dickens, fifty-four years earlier, first saw wind-swept or fog-clouded skies above his head. But the particular Wells who haunts us today was born a generation later than his birthdate. It is the idealistic young tutor of biology who "collapsed into literary journalism," who wrote *The Time Machine* and *The First Men on the Moon,* whose step is light and brisk. The ghost had earned godfatherly privileges at one of the rebirths of "science-fiction." Imaginary voyages into space, aided by enthusiastic use of the telescope, were notorious and fashionable adventures as early as the seventeenth century. The eighteenth century was not unaware of them; yet the more famous journeys, Defoe's *A New Voyage round the World,* and *Robinson Crusoe* and notably Swift's *Travels by Lemuel Gulliver* chose water as their element. The romances of Jules Verne came earlier than Wells's ventures, but Wells, more brilliantly versed in latter-day popular science than Verne, returned to models provided by Swift and Defoe. Wells's romances, like Defoe's, had the air of being documentary reports, and like

Swift's they were parables of life on earth, or rather of life, as far as Wells could discern it, within the complicated, minutely class-divided structure of English society. Wells's inspiration for *The Time Machine* began with a paper he wrote to demonstrate the existence of the fourth dimension, the "Universe Rigid," a stiff, self-conscious essay in popular science which was rejected by Frank Harris, the deep-voiced, black-haired editor of the *Fortnightly Review*. The fourth dimension was "news" in the 1890's; any mention of it awakened the same curiosity that talk about "relativity" had thirty years ago. It was necessary for Wells to give that topic "life,". to give it human relevance, to make his theory felt as well as understood. He solved his problem by converting it into a parable of what might happen if British society were divided into two races: those who ran machines, lived underground, and were scarcely human; and those who lived on the surface of the earth, beautiful, indulged, nearly witless creatures whose voices slurred into musical phrases, all dependent on the labors of their underground slaves, helpless in the presence of machines, and all living, not without fear, in a sunset glow of civilization.

The actual force of Wells's parable developed in terms of social meaning rather than of scientific revelation. Was this social satire? Perhaps; one could read it that way. Was it Swiftian in speculation of human destiny? No; it lacked Swift's nearly tragic vision of human savagery—and lacked Swift's whiplash, his passionate hatred of human folly. Wells's vision was one of warning, because Wells believed that human beings would listen to warnings—if their minds were freed. This belief is at the center of Wells's famous liberalism; it also defines the character of his no less famous optimism. "Freedom of mind" with the security of peace around it, the peace of Plato's idealism, the middle world of ideas in which mankind realized concepts of divine origin defined the Utopia Wells held in view. The parable of *The First Men on the Moon* contains the same hope. At the end of the book, Cavor—the scientist from earth held captive by the creatures of the moon—who establishes communication with the earth from his prison on the moon, is killed by his captors. Unwisely he allowed moon's creatures to learn earth's ambitions toward empire building, to conquer the universe by force, by war. Moon's creatures then found no other alternative but to destroy him, to cut themselves off from barbarous earth. Wells's effort was to warn his readers that wars were held in disrepute by all possible forms of living intelligence except mankind's. *The First Men on the Moon* was published in 1901, the moment when the people of Western civilization held greatest hope for the promises of a new world opening up to them in the progress of a "scientific" twentieth century.

Readers of science-fiction today may find *The Time Machine* and Wells's voyage to the moon tame, less highly seasoned than recent romances of the same genre. Science-fiction, as we know it now, is the popular, dubiously legitimate, sub-subconscious offspring of violence in current fiction. Its greatest revival came during and after World War II. Its narrative patterns followed earlier designs of the gangster and western romance—its hidden forces, its dehumanized human elements are those of sadistic encounters and destruction. Readers who might be ashamed of (or afraid of) being too strongly attracted by scenes of violence in other forms of literature could accept science-fiction as instructive of future life on the far shores of an "expanding universe." How deliberately the writers of science-fiction follow wild west-gangster formulas I do not know; the greatest possibility is that the science-fiction writer is not the cynical monster he so often appears to be, but that he has the same hidden enjoyment of thrills and terror which delights the science-fiction reader. This is the secret which is shared between them. Beneath the surfaces of recent science-fiction, totalitarian and atomic warfare mount the skies in technicolor profusion; fear of the future is among the dominant emotions awakened by nuclear fission—and if one looks for parables within science-fiction, one finds that they point toward victories of a "one-world," totalitarian drive to power.

The distance between Wellsian science-fiction and its present revivals can be measured by recognizing two extremes of fear: in Wells's books the fear is that mankind will carry into the future its past mistakes, and Wells's warning implies a rejection of the past. The more thoughtful science-fiction writers of the 1950's face a more explosive, more lethal, darker future than Wells had in mind, nor do they seem as confident as he did that their warnings can clear, if not purify, the air. This distinction is, I think, important. A dark aura encircles the fantasies of Arthur C. Clarke who is perhaps the youngest, and certainly the best, of writers in a genre that even today has renewed inspiration from *The Time Machine*. Like the writings of the early Wells, Clarke's short stories and romances are less easy to dismiss as merely science-fiction than the work of his fellow craftsmen. Like Wells of *The First Men on the Moon,* the weight of his prose is light, the structure of his stories neat and polished; he is obviously the latest "master" in his chosen genre. His book of stories, *Reach for Tomorrow,* has a variety which extends from the psychological sharpness of "The Parasite" to the topical wit of "Jupiter Five"; it is the first time in many years that John Collier of *Fancies and Goodnights* has had a rival. Under any name or title Clarke's fiction is a delight to read. But the paradox produced by reading too many of Clarke's interstellar space romances is intellectual claustrophobia. One's mind is locked in a future of totalitarian doom. Human loyalties to place and to other human creatures vanish—these are the dark auras of Clarke's wit and inventiveness. Clarke's mad, power-driven scientists are successful; while Wells's devotees of science, equally mad, pay the price for their logical deductions with their lives.

The distinction that Wells's science-fiction has, and why *The Time Machine* is still unique with a timelessness of its own, is that Wells held at the center of his writings a protest against darkness—intellectual darkness—and in his science-fiction, however out of fashion it may fall, the protest has a resounding note. To clear away the darkness of the past was Wells's effort; to the young H. G. Wells scientific knowledge and inventiveness were the means of leaving Victorian darkness—or any other darkness—in the shadows behind him. If his best writings have an air of "cleanliness" it is because his mind fought the claustrophobia of Victorian lower (very low) middle-class poverty, of group thinking (within a short time he found himself at odds with the Fabians), and, when he had become famous enough to be invited out to dinner, of London literary circles.

2

His *Experiment in Autobiography* (1934) is not the book that it might have been—the fully annotated document of a Victorian-Edwardian literary career, a "success story" of one of the highest paid literary journalists in England, the man who came from nowhere and who for thirty years influenced, and often guided, the liberal thinking of the twentieth century. The first two hundred pages of Wells's *Experiment* are as remarkable as the author himself; yet a warning of the thinness, like that of skimmed-milk prose, which diluted the latter four hundred-odd pages to round-table discussions wearily circulating at two in the morning, is in the book's subtitle, "Discoveries and Conclusions of a Very Ordinary Brain." This was not modesty, nor irony; it was part of Wells's liberal belief that a "very ordinary brain" was one to be valued and respected; yet the phrase has a deeper meaning. Wells grew easily bored at writing about himself, or rather that side of himself which did not preside at a public meeting. And the truth was that the memorable scenes of the first two hundred pages, which included portraits of his mother and father—his mother, educated as a Victorian lady's maid, his father as a country gentleman's gardener—had been written before, but disguised as fiction, in his novel, *Tono-Bungay*. The best of the autobiographical Wells is in that novel, his masterpiece of social comedy. If one may speak of "light prose" with something of the same meaning that we speak of "light verse," *Tono-Bungay* has a place of its own in British fiction. But one must distinguish it from the comedy of Dickens' half-Gothic, poetic prose, the hilarity of comic scenes in his major novels. One must also remove it from the vicinity of Evelyn Waugh's wit—that is of another vintage. Thackeray's *Vanity Fair* is of no nearer kinship; it has taken nearly fifty years to recognize *Tono-Bungay*'s Edwardian-Wellsian high spirits as another approach to the vanities of Western civilization, nor has the advertising genius of Ponderevo, Wells's chemist who invented "Tono-Bungay," declined; it has grown to much larger proportions in the United States. It is the genius that makes presidential campaigns "the greatest shows on earth" flickering and roaring from TV screens. The new word for it is "publicity."

None of Wells's fiction withstands the test of rereading as admirably as *Tono-Bungay;* it is not merely Wells's best book, it is an Edwardian masterpiece; it has the abundance of the Victorian "three-decker" and yet it is "streamlined" within scarcely four hundred pages. In its own day (1909) it bridged the distance between "the problem novel" and the novel of ideas. Like the novels of E. M. Forster, its argumentative brilliance prepared the way for the intellectual content of D. H. Lawrence's *Women in Love* and the early novels of Aldous Huxley. Beyond its own *Zeitgeist, Tono-Bungay* still opens the door to the largest booth of the twentieth-century's "Vanity Fair" where advertising—the faked poetry of successful careers, industry, and politics ("the poetry of commerce" Wells called it)—is bought and sold. It is significant that Ponderevo, the mock hero-villain of the book, rises from the lower middle classes only to burst in mid-air; he does not escape his doom. The civilization that made his rise possible also had the power to destroy him, to leave him on his deathbed, the victim of an ability to make "quick money." The point is that Ponderevo is trapped by the values he tried to manipulate; he is the inflated "little man," who a generation later was to become Germany's Hitler and France's Laval. Was Wells too mild in making him a comic figure? I think not. He is a figure of Anglo-American derivation; it is better to keep him true to his origins, and to remember that though an analogy to his failure can be drawn from his European heirs, he is seen in the perspective of his own environment. The distinctive features of democracy, with its heritage of parliamentary government, keep our Ponderevos, no matter how large they grow, within range of comic reference.

Ponderevo's nephew and biographer is the thinly disguised, autobiographical Wells, the Wells who sought for "freedom and trackless ways," who very nearly, but not quite, confused definitions of "truth" with those of "science," and felt that beyond art or literature, his duty was to reach toward truth into "the heart of life," to "disentangle" it and to make it "clear."

But as Wells reached toward his "reality," the search was beyond himself, and with loyalty to his Platonic liberalism (though his relationships with women were more ardent, irritable, and paradoxically lonely than Platonic) the view was often beyond visible horizons. During his boyhood his claustrophobia had a hint of agoraphobia in it. Like Trollope's at Harrow, Wells's boyhood humiliations, his poverty, were strongly associated with a world of country houses where he had small rights, if any, to exist. That world was governed (through the grace of his mother) by a Low Church Victorian God. Though the prospect was as delightful as landscapes that Jane Austen knew, Wells was consciously blind to it—and for good reasons. His place was so "low" that the loveliest, broadest landscape turned to desert; yet it would be wrong to say that Wells forgot it; it returns in a vision of the future in *The Time*

Machine; it is a "condemned playground" of flowers, grasses, and Liberal gentry, country houses fallen into charming ruins, peopled by creatures "on the intellectual level of . . . five-year-old children" and condemned because of outmoded childish fancies and fears. Was Wells deliberate in this reconstruction—in ruins—of Kentish Up Park where his mother served as housekeeper? He may have been; but it would have been unlike him to turn that deliberation inward to brood upon it; meanwhile the boy, and later the "bright young man," spent his waking hours looking for an escape from a world he knew too well.

Whatever may be said about the culture of late Victorian England it opened several doors at the top of a stairway to an H. G. Wells. The largest was labeled "Trade"; the others were "Politics," "Tutoring," "Popular Science," and "Journalism." Art, literature, law, and higher branches of the teaching as well as scientific professions and the Church were jealously reserved (as everyone knew) for those who had attended Public School and the two universities, Oxford and Cambridge. And British culture with its romantic acceptance of world empire as well as a popular notion of evolution, was decidedly eclectic. The failure of his father's shopkeeping closed the door of trade to Wells; for this "bright young man" business was a trap, or rather, the risk of failure in it was too obvious, too clear. The other four doors were less hazardous, more attractive; he retained his interest in politics, and combined the usefulness of the latter three: first as apprentice, in a chemist's shop, then as a teaching-scholarship boy, then as tutoring student at the Imperial College of Science and Technology at the Univerity of London, and last as journalist for scientific publications. Wells had no illusions concerning the merits of any class or the need of class distinctions. In England he knew that class hierarchies of the Victorian-Edwardian order were rapidly slipping into the past and he noted that decline in his many novels. Unlike George Orwell of a later generation, his liberalism contained no illusions guided by the promises of Marx; therefore he did not share the disillusionment of the latter-day liberal journalists who had followed him.

Wells's independence was that of the aboriginal British islander, overlaid with the hatred of the Anglo-Saxon for Norman rule. He was a rare British republican with no respect for the Crown. This kind of independence made Wells distrust the promises made by the elite, whether they came from the lips of Fabians, Beatrice and Sidney Webb (he saw Sidney Webb as a good civil servant, but no more), or the lips of Lenin. In spite of his vision of a world state, his spirit was the same as the island English who manned boats and ships at the evacuation of Dunkirk and Dieppe in World War II. The evacuation of British troops across the Channel was the work of thousands who had "ordinary" brains, and their accomplishment converted a military disaster into a civilian and island victory.

And last, what of Wells's literary position? Journalism engulfed it and that he knew as well as any of his critics. In his famous quarrel with Henry James (since he could not eat his cake and reserve the crumbs for art) he took the side of journalism versus art, a position held by his predecessor, the arch-Conservative Kipling as well as his contemporary, the pro-Roman-Church journalist, G. K. Chesterton. The position had no taint of compromise as far as art was mentioned. If James was a snob, Wells stood committed as a Philistine: that was the score. Yet his position had more candor, more sturdiness, and was of tougher moral fiber than those held by Hugh Walpole and Arnold Bennett, the two writers of popular fiction who in their day seemed to rival Wells. Both flirted with art. Both had the journalist's ear and eye for what the public of Edwardian taste would care to read; they were happy victims of a *Zeitgeist* that gave them immediate rewards. Their flirtations with art could not extend their fame, nor could the skills of craftsmanship endure beyond the moment of their deaths. Bennett's *The*

Old Wives' Tale remains a somber trophy of "what a writer he might have been!" And Henry James's favored novelist in a large group of younger writers was Hugh Walpole, who is remembered best in a biography that deserves to be cherished by more readers than have discovered it: *Hugh Walpole* by Rupert Hart-Davies. Of Wells's contemporaries among the Fabians, only Bernard Shaw ("a raw, aggressive Dubliner" Wells called him) survives the wreckage of an era—but then Shaw had too much wit to flirt with art. When the necessity came for him to use art, he embraced it as though he held a willing actress in his arms in the glare of footlights on the stage. Shaw being Anglo-Irish, and of no place at all either high or low in the British hierarchy of classes, could afford, though poor enough at the beginning of his career in London, a recklessly shabby, genteel, aristocratic air, the prerogative of a foreigner who wrote with a purity of diction that few of his London, or Oxford, contemporaries could command.

As far as his writing can carry us, the living Wells is preserved for us in three books, the first published in 1895, the last in 1909, *The Time Machine, The First Men on the Moon* and *Tono-Bungay*. The voluminous other writings are likely to collect dust rather than cause a resurrection of the spirit. His Platonic idea that men could be better than they were still haunts the middle streams of British culture, where, incidentally, the sharp distinctions of Britain's upper middle class have been swept away. Since World War II Britain's internal social revolutions have followed a Wellsian model rather than the Marxian pattern of open class warfare, and the household servant class which his mother represented has disappeared. In America, the spread of Wellsian liberal idealism has taken a less political, but no less characteristic, form. It hangs like a rosy mist whenever and wherever heads of large corporations meet to create new foundations for the giving of grants "for culture." On its material side it retains Ponderevo's faith in the "poetry of commerce"—now called publicity—and relief from income taxes; in the United States the representatives of Wellsian liberalism are often millionaires. But Wells's restless campaign for enlightenment could never be represented by a firebrand held high against the night. Wells's torch is a rod of neon light, unaesthetic as you please, a common fixture, diffusing rays upward against passing clouds in a hopeful sky.

George Moore and Regionalism in Realistic Fiction

IN AMERICA, THE LITERARY FASHIONS of the 1880's and the 1890's which had been imported from continental Europe and its islands, enjoyed an obscure old age until the years immediately following the first World War. This has been particularly true of our relations to British literature of *Yellow Book* origins and to the tradition of Flaubert, and in this respect we have been slower than the Germans. Someone—I believe it was D. H. Lawrence—said that Thomas Mann was "the last sick sufferer from the complaint of Flaubert," but Flaubert was not generally appreciated as a serious novelist in the United States until 1919! By that time, we had belatedly discovered George Moore—and not the George Moore who has always and still deserves a measure of our attention, but he who had written *Confessions of a Young Man,* the George Moore who had so flagrantly enjoyed the liberties he had taken in writing and re-editing his dead life. We embraced his foolishness, his indiscretions; and we shared vicariously, of course, his love of shocking those who were supposedly a shade more innocent than he. We enjoyed half-seriously his belated impersonations of Huysmans, Pater, Wilde, and Gautier—but admiration of this kind grew chilly beyond the third decade of

125

the present century, and at the moment of his death in 1933, his literary remains had begun to fall, soundlessly and with scant honors, into the semiobscurity in which they rest today.

If one makes allowances for the slight embarrassments which attend a revival of recently outmoded literary figures, a re-reading of George Moore's early novels is by no means difficult. The only difficulty that arises is the possible mistake of taking their author too seriously, but one does not stop reading; something is there that outlives the moment of its creation. One decides to follow the heroine of *A Mummer's Wife* to her last fifth of gin in a London slum, one pauses to take another look and not without amusement) at Lewis Seymour in *A Modern Lover* boldly posed naked (he was to represent a dancing faun) in Mrs. Bentham's drawing room. One then recalls how swiftly and how skillfully Moore introduced the latest fashions in French naturalism to the subscribers of London's circulating libraries. This was in the early 1880's and at a moment when the very thought of translating Zola into English for the enlightenment of the British public seemed both highly experimental and morally dangerous. Perhaps a reason why the libraries (after a brief dispute) decided to accept Moore was that it must have been as difficult to take Moore seriously then as it is today. Moore earnestly defended his lack of humor, but the spirit which his early books convey has the charm, the occasional turn of brilliant observation, the eagerness, the sensitivity of the obviously immature, yet gifted writer.

One agrees that the circulating libraries took small risk in allowing *A Modern Lover* and *A Mummer's Wife* to pass from hand to hand among young British matrons or their house-maids. The books may well have been shocking, but the incidents that were artfully contrived to shock us are so innocently, so boyishly confided and so lightly placed and stressed, they had the air of being "entertainments," rather than the weighted arguments that would blast the family hearth or endanger the Stock Exchange. Despite the skill with which Moore handled the formulas of naturalism, despite his exact descriptions of airless and shabby rooms or fog-darkened streets, his scenes of Paris and of London lack emotional reality, quite as they lack the realities of verbal warmth and density and color. It was not until his third novel was written, *A Drama in Muslin*, in 1886, that one could possibly discern a third-dimensional quality at work; there, the scene is well within the English pale of Ireland, and is circumscribed by journeys to and from Dublin's viceregal court, the parlors of the Shelbourne Hotel, and Anglo-Irish estates and country houses.

Since I believe that George Moore was indisputably an Irish writer rather than an Irishman who had acquired British poise, the occasion arises for a brief commentary on the regional aspects of naturalism in fiction. One should not be surprised to find Moore at his best on Irish soil, for the premise of his consciously acquired art (the realistic novel in its latest form) almost demanded that he should have been, but before I enlarge upon the Anglo-Irish character of Moore's work, what seems both a truism and a paradox in the esthetics of realism should be given a hearing.

The realistic novel, as we have known it, is of protean shapes; it is of many tongues and of many varieties, depths, and colors. It is easy to agree that Fielding, Gogol, Tolstoy, Balzac, Flaubert, Dickens, Nexö, Dreiser, and the Thomas Mann who wrote his *Buddenbrooks* were realistic novelists. The mask that realism wears is international and yet the hidden limitations of the realistic novel are regional. The best and most far-reaching examples of its art depend upon an intimate awareness of a particular environment; the particulars of human behavior present their immediate problems to the author and reader alike, for both must feel the external truth of what is being said and done. It has taken a second World War with its news of a northeastern front extending into the far reaches of the Russian plains to endow Tolstoy's *War and Peace* with a renewed vitality for the American reader. And those readers who cannot carry in the mind's eye the omnipresent, yellow-gray density of fog in nineteenth-century London would also fail to grasp the full meaning of the theme and its variations in Dickens' masterpiece, *Bleak House*. As one follows the mutations of realism and its heirs in the novels of Zola in France, of George Moore in Ireland, of Dreiser, Sherwood Anderson, and James T. Farrell in the American Middle West, the writer's awareness of a particular time and place seems to increase; he tends to grow more and more dependent upon the realities of an environment and a region that he knows well, and with this knowledge, he conveys the strength of his convictions to his reader. To the foreign reader he demands an effort in the direction of an accurate translation—and lacking that effort, the best of his serious writing is likely to become transformed into a novel of exotic charm, as though it were a trip to a strange place, in which the wilds of urban Chicago, New York, or Paris, may assume (to the reader's eye) the same attraction that is felt in reading an account of a journey to the source of an unknown river in Brazil. In this sense, many a realistic novel offers the blandishments of an "escape" for the bored or harried reader; and, often enough, the very rich have enjoyed the exotic charms of a novel relating the misfortunes of the very poor.

George Moore's eager and enthusiastic practice of the arts of realism, even today, has an air of seeming fresh and adventurous. He did not seem to move at a measured pace, but to leap and to dive, swimming through gaps in his own inventions by hasty adaptations of scenes and episodes from the novels of Flaubert and Zola; the water was cold, but he churned its surface until it sparkled. If the successes of *A Modern Lover* and *A Mummer's Wife* did not bring him fame, they suddenly illuminated the curious aura of notoriety that was always to be associated with the mention of his name; and the phenomenon deceived a number of his critics, Virginia Woolf among them, into thinking that his gifts were exclusively those which enabled him to write his fictional autobiographies; and there is little to show that he himself was not equally deceived, for George Moore, as his *Confessions* and his *Memoirs of My Dead Life* so plainly testify, was unable to make a clear distinction between notoriety and fame. A transitory burst of candor meant as much to him as an arduous search for truth, and he mistook the surprise he caused by the first for the more difficult achievements of the latter. It was candor that betrayed Moore's lack of true worldliness; and his confidences, whispered aloud for all the world to hear ("Moore never kissed but told"), left him naked to the rebukes of his more seriously minded contemporaries. Bernard Shaw's stage directions and prefaces to his plays even when they had the air of taking the reader or spectator into personal confidence, never failed of their objective in social criticism; in Moore's voice, the personal aside was less clearly directed and controlled, and however often it ridiculed the canons of Victorian respectability, it frequently lapsed into what seemed to be the utterance of a deliberately phrased faux pas.

But between the writing of his first two novels and his *Confessions of a Young Man,* Moore wrote the earliest of three books that merit our attention. *A Drama in Muslin,* and, as if to strengthen and support any argument that Moore's work was at its happiest at home, the book was actually written in Ireland. The training he had received in Paris (for the city of Paris had been his university and Manet, Turgenev, and Zola may be regarded as his instructors) began to bear the fruits of his industry. Within ten years he had been transformed from an Anglo-Irish dilettante, born to an estate that yielded several hundreds of pounds per annum, into an industrious novelist and man of letters—and in Dublin he possessed the advantage gained by a lack of celebrity at home. If in a later generation, Joyce saw the Dublin of his *Ulysses* with a steadier and more deeply penetrating eye than Moore, we should remember that Moore was there before him, viewing the city with a gaze of youthful detachment and a true concern for the arts of prose.

In *A Drama in Muslin,* Moore's acknowledged spokesman is a Mr. John Harding, a novelist, who drifts, almost unseen, through Dublin streets and through the reception rooms of the Shelbourne Hotel; he is an object of admiration for Moore's plain-featured, shy, and humorless little heroine, Alice Barton, but the admiration does not grow into love, for Mr. Harding remains her self-appointed guardian and educator.

In rereading *A Drama in Muslin* one half envies those who discovered Moore as a promising young novelist in the 1880's; as in *A Modern Lover* and *A Mummer's Wife* his lack of maturity was again turned to his advantage; and even today, one feels that his sensibilities heralded the awakening of a new spirit in modern fiction. The marriage market of an Anglo-Irish gentry at Dublin's viceregal court was the object of Moore's concern and ironic observation; the court is gone, and the immediate occasion for Moore's protest against the fate of innocent and badly educated young men and women, paired off and sold at the marriage market by ambitious mothers and bankrupt fathers has long since passed. But to view sex clearly as a marketable social commodity was a position taken up by Bernard Shaw a few years later in *Mrs. Warren's Profession,* and the close juxtapositions of extreme wealth and extreme poverty which created so much dramatic and intellectual excitement in Shaw's early plays have their première in *A Drama in Muslin.* If Turgenev had read and admired Maria Edgeworth and learned from her a measure of the skill required in writing a realistic novel of social irony, Moore had been no less assiduous in taking hints from Turgenev's discoveries in reading *Castle Rackrent* and *The Absentee.* An inspired cycle of literary apprenticeships had come to a full round and returned to its source within the English pale in Ireland. But Moore's sensibilities were also tuned to receive all the protests of a youthful generation that had been caught in the net of elderly ambitions, mistakes, and Victorian hypocrisies. It is not just to say that Moore lacked art in the writing of *A Drama in*

Muslin; yet its atmosphere of something we call an artless charm pervades throughout the narrative; we enjoy it in much the same spirit that we find pleasure in witnessing an earnest and enthusiastic rehearsal of a play in a small town six weeks before its arrival ten doors west of Broadway; the director is inspired and is willing to risk a few experiments in technique that an older and perhaps wiser man would consciously avoid and the actors are doing better (if one makes allowances for awkward pauses and incompleted gestures) than they know. The episodic and simultaneous shift of scene between a land-owner bargaining with rebellious tenants, and his wife bargaining for the sale of their pretty daughter is a venture into the experimental techniques of realistic fiction that has been continued from the day *A Drama in Muslin* first appeared to the writing of John Dos Passos' *The 42nd Parallel.* The characters of Mrs. Barton, the scheming mother, who learns too late the feminine unwisdom of turning each rival mother with a girl for sale into an enemy, the stupid beauty, her daughter Olive, her husband, the landlord who fancies himself a painter of unrecognized talents, the young Lord Kilcarney, the "catch" of the Dublin season, who is besieged alike by rapacious mothers and starving tenants, are memorably and sensitively drawn. Moore's improvisions were those of an exceptionally bright student of realistic fiction who had suddenly usurped the master's place and had become for one brief hour the teacher, and if not the philosopher, the guide. In sensibility he had advanced beyond all other younger novelists of his day; only the mature Henry James with his virtually unread and certainly unappreciated *Princess Casamassima* overshadowed him, and in the position he had won, he attained a freedom of eloquence and a quickness of perception which in many of his later novels and in their numerous revisions were either stilled or blotted from the page.

In *A Drama in Muslin* he had found almost too much to say

on too many varied subjects, but all were related to his discontent of living in Ireland:

> The Dublin streets stare the vacant and helpless stare of a beggar selling matches on a doorstep. . . . On either side of you, there is bawling ignorance or plaintive decay. . . . We are in a land of echoes and shadows. . . . Is there a girl or young man in Dublin who has read a play of Shakespeare, a novel of Balzac, a poem of Shelley? Is there one who could say for certain that Leonardo da Vinci, was neither a comic-singer or patriot?—No. Like children, the young and old, run hither and thither, seeking in Liddell oblivion of the Land League. Catholic in name, they curse the Pope for not helping them in their affliction; moralists by tradition, they accept at their parties women who parade their lovers to the town from the top of a tramcar. In Dublin there is baptism in tea and communion in a cutlet.

The discontent that Moore displayed was salutary and one feels that he expressed it with deeper penetration into the lives of a people than the kind of social criticism he had to offer later in the pages of *Esther Waters* and *Evelyn Innes*. One does not easily forget the scene in which the weak and bewildered Lord Kilcarney wanders alone on the stone embankments of the Liffey in the small dark hours of the morning, pursued by promises of ambitious mothers with marriageable daughters and harried by threats of economic ruin promised with equal vehemence by Parnell and the Land League.

Looking backward and in that glance reviewing the social dramas of Bernard Shaw, the pamphlets and speeches of the Fabian Society, the domestic novels of Arnold Bennett, and the H. G. Wells of *Mr. Polly* and *Tono-Bungay,* the flashes of youthful insight which illuminate the narrative of *A Drama in Muslin* seem at this distance to have acquired the prophetic intonations of a Delphic oracle. As the novel closes, one reads the following description of Ashbourne Crescent in London:

> To some this air of dull well-to-do-ness may seem as intolerable, as obscene in its way as the look of melancholy silliness which the Dub-

liners and their dirty city wear so unintermittently. One is the inevitable decay which must precede an outburst of national energy; the other is the smug optimism, that fund of materialism, on which a nation lives, and which in truth represents the bulwarks wherewith civilisation defends itself against those sempiternal storms which like atmospheric convulsions, by destroying, renew the tired life of man. And that Ashbourne Crescent, with its bright brass knockers, its white-capped maidservant, and spotless oilcloths, will in the dim future pass away before some great tide of revolution that is now gathering strength far away, deep down and out of sight in the heart of the nation, is probable enough; but it is certainly now, in all its cheapness and vulgarity, more than anything else representative, though the length and breadth of the land be searched, of the genius of Empire that has been glorious through the long tale that nine hundred years have to tell. . . .

It is in Ashbourne Crescent that Moore's solemn and candid heroine became a successful lady novelist and it was there, happily wedded to a physician, that she came to rest; the comedy was over, and Moore's little study in social irony had a satisfactory and plausible conclusion.

Moore's return to Ireland at the end of the century (as everyone who has read his *Hail and Farewell* remembers) had been inspired by W. B. Yeats's enthusiasm and his urgent propaganda for a Celtic Renaissance in literature. By this time Moore's celebrity in London was well established, and the temperamental differences which always existed and were never resolved between the two men, had been shrewdly put aside by Yeats with the purpose of using Moore's gifts and notoriety to support a worthy cause. I happen to believe that Yeats's invitation came to Moore at a critical moment in his career, that it prolonged his creative life by another decade, and we, as readers of Moore's half-forgotten novels, are enriched by a rediscovery of *The Lake* and *The Untilled Field*. Among Moore's weaknesses as a mature writer (and despite his industry) was his infinite capacity for being bored; the boredom was all the more insidious because Moore lacked sufficient self-knowledge to realize its effect upon his work. The curse of dullness which is so brilliantly absent from his early novels and his scenes of life in Ireland, begins its round in the pages of *Esther Waters* and is resumed after the completion of *Hail and Farewell* to continue till the end of his life which closed so inauspiciously with *Aphrodite in Aulis* and *The Pastoral Loves of Daphnis and Chloe* and *Peronnik the Fool*. When Yeats's invitation came, Moore had the need to be prodded back to the centers of his discontent, to be made aware of them in such fashion that his active sensibilities could be reawakened. I am not prepared to say that Yeats fully perceived the importance of his urgent invitation to George Moore; I suspect not, I suspect that he was too deeply concerned with his own relationship to the Celtic Renaissance to realize that he had granted Moore more than a passing favor. I am inclined to believe that their subsequent quarrels had at their source an aesthetic (and therefore far less flagrantly personal) cause of disagreement than certain passages in *Hail and Farewell* and Yeats's *Dramatis Personae* would seem to indicate. Moore was an excellently intuitive and sensitive critic of modern painting while Yeats was a notably inept one; Moore was a naively schooled and indifferent critic of verse which his *Anthology of Pure Poetry* proved to all the world, while Yeats in his own voice as a poet commanded an authority that was and still remains superior to almost everything that Moore might have to say concerning poetry. It is impossible to speak of Yeats's work without acknowledging the far reach inward to the realities of subjective being while the delights of reading Moore's prose are those which are gained by reading the observations of a man who has been inspired by the presence of an active world around him.

But whatever the causes of Moore's reawakening of energy may have been, the stories which Moore included in *The Untilled Field* remain as fresh today as in the hour that he wrote them to be translated into Irish in 1900. The spirit in which he composed them was cheerfully stressed in his preface to the Carra Edition of *The Untilled Field* in 1923:

> . . . I wrote "The Wedding Gown," "Alms Giving," "The Clerk's Quest," and "So On He Fares," in English rather than in Anglo-Irish, for of what help would that pretty idiom, in which we catch the last accents of the original language, be to Tiagh Donoghue, my translator? . . . but these first stories begot a desire to paint the portrait of my country, and this could only be done in a Catholic atmosphere. . . . "The Exile" rose up in my mind quickly, and before putting the finishing hand to it I began "Home Sickness." The village of Duncannon in the story set me thinking of the villages around Dublin, and I wrote "Some Parishioners," "Patchwork," "The Wedding Feast," and "The Window." The somewhat harsh rule of Father Maguire set me thinking of a gentler type of priest, and the pathetic figure of Father MacTurnan tempted me. I wrote "A Letter to Rome" and "A Play-House in the Waste"; and as fast as these stories were written they were translated into Irish. . . .

With the aid of a literal translation (done by T. W. Rolleston) of a few of the stories back into their original English, Moore edited *The Untilled Field* for British and American publication; Gaelic imagery had strengthened the original text, and the stories were, as he wrote, "much improved by their bath in Irish. 'She had a face such as one sees in a fox' . . . how much better than 'She had a fox-like face.' "

The little stories, sketches, and a novelette, "The Wild Goose" which are listed in the contents of *The Untilled Field* were never widely read, and Moore himself confessed that he had half-forgotten their existence because he was so soon engaged in writing a sequel to them in *The Lake*. Perhaps the lack of appreciation they received injured Moore's vanity, but it is more likely that coming as they did from a semiconscious source of inspiration Moore underrated their importance, and presented them with a display of too much modesty. Something of their true quality is suggested in the speech of the anonymous spectator who tells the story of the blind man in "Alms-Giving:"

> The new leaves were beginning in the high branches. I was sitting where sparrows were building their nests, and very soon I seemed to see further into life than I had ever seen before. "We're here," I said, "for the purpose of learning what life is, and the blind beggar has taught me a great deal, something that I could not have learnt out of a book, a deeper truth than any book contains. . . ."

In this spirit Moore created his Father Maguire, the stupidly domineering priest, and Father MacTurnan, the innocent and heroically humane father of his parish and with them there is the remarkable Biddy M'Hale who caused Father Maguire so much trouble by donating the money for a window in his new church and following her, there is the story of "The Wild Goose," the repatriated Anglo-Irish newspaperman, whose career as a politician in Ireland has its broad analogy to the career of Parnell, and among the best of the shorter pieces is "The Wedding Gown" in which Moore's sensibility reminds one of the qualities that are discovered in rereading the tales of Hans Christian Andersen. In his introduction to the Carra Edition of *The Untilled Field,* it was characteristic of the later Moore to claim that his Irish stories served as a precedent for John Synge's *The Playboy of the Western World,* but whether they did or not (and I suspect that they did not) the quality of their prose and the sensitivity of their observations foreshadowed the writing of Joyce's *Dubliners. The Untilled Field* contains no story as well controlled or as delicately contrived as Joyce's little masterpiece, "The Dead," but the reaches of *The Untilled Field* closely approximate the intentions and accomplishments of Joyce's stories, and with the exceptions of Joyce's "The Dead" and "A Little Cloud," Moore's stories are markedly superior.

To us who read Moore at a trans-Atlantic distance and at a time when his once-spectacular introduction of literary modes

and attitudes seem outworn, an interesting and seemingly
farfetched analogy—a parallel, if you will—between George
Moore and Sherwood Anderson comes to mind. For a moment,
the parallel seems curious rather than exact, but the more I
think of it, the closer the work of the two writers falls together,
and the analogy which seemed to span too great a distance
between them reveals something that results in a just understanding and estimate of their contributions, each separately,
to a national literature.

Like Moore, Anderson indulged himself in a wealth of
semi-autobiographical reminiscence and extolled the merits of
candor above those of truth, and like Moore's autobiographies,
Anderson's memoirs and storyteller's stories seem less like
actual confessions than works of fiction that had been released
from the disciplines employed by writing a short story or a
novel. To a notable degree both men as writers lost themselves
among the high arches and corridors of the palace of art. In
later life, Moore returned to his early and ill-advised worship
of Walter Pater, and his habits of industry kept him chained
to the task of writing the books which now seemed fated for
oblivion. With equal misfortune, Anderson's love of the perfect phrase, the prose sentence, and paragraph that remain an
eternal delight to the eye and ear seems to have sterilized the
gifts that promised so brilliant a future in the two volumes of
his short stories, *Winesburg, Ohio* and *The Triumph of the
Egg.* If Moore's source of inspiration lay within the English
pale surrounding Dublin, certainly the sources of the sensibilities that Anderson so memorably expressed may be found
within an equally small circumference of Midwestern small
towns, railway junctions, and farm lands; and the resemblance
between the work of the two men increases as one remembers
the debt that a younger generation of writers owed to them.
To the same degree that *A Drama in Muslin, The Untilled
Field,* and *The Lake* anticipated the discernments of a new
literary generation in Anglo-Irish—and indeed, British—lit-

erature, Anderson's early short stories preceded the now familiar complex of youthful sensibility and a concern for artful presentation, of naturalism and of individual candor that is so strongly marked in the early writings of Hemingway, Faulkner, and Dos Passos. Both elder writers possessed the impulse "to see further into life," something that could not be learned out of a book and was "a deeper truth than any book contains." This impulse is, of course, by no means an uncommon impulse in any generation, but Moore's and Anderson's discovery and expression of it, set an example for the young writers who came after them.

It would be easy to regard Moore's long career in writing prose a failure, and it is certainly easy for me to repeat that the expectations he awakened were never quite fulfilled, that the very terms of his art (those of the naturalistic novel) left him discontented, that he never perceived fully the richness and value of his Irish origins even as they were displayed in his own writing. The almost fatal lack of knowing fully his true identity with Ireland cut him off from those sources of feeling which might have resulted in work of lesser scope than he enjoyed, and would have been of more mature and lasting satisfaction. Easy as it may be to enlarge his failures and dimmed as Moore's reputation is today, the scales of a final judgment still tip in his favor. I have repeatedly spoken of his sensibility, and I have done so because everything he wrote reflects the writer whose art is guided by feeling rather than the deeper inward reaches of emotion. Few writers survive the trials of writing their autobiographies—a last farewell that should be taken late in life—and Moore, after his confessions and memoirs of a dead life, retained enough energy to write his third and best, *Hail and Farewell,* which overshadowed the merits of his more pretentious novels. The sensibility of which I speak had its moments of a significant hold on the imagination and its presence distinguishes Moore from all other writers of prose in English who suffered the transition which carried them from the nineteenth century into the twentieth. One thinks of Moore's survival in much the same terms as Father Oliver's swim to safety in the closing pages of *The Lake*:

> A long mile of water lay between him and Joycetown, but there was a courage he had never felt before in his heart, and a strength he had never felt before in his limbs. Once he stood up in the water, sorry that the crossing was not longer. "Perhaps I shall have had enough of it before I get there"; and he turned on his side and swam half a mile before changing his stroke. He changed it and got on his back because he was beginning to feel cold and tired, and soon after he began to think that it would be about as much as he could do to reach the shore. A little later he was swimming frog-fashion, but the change did not seem to rest him, and seeing the shore still a long way off he began to think that perhaps after all he would find his end in the lake. His mind set on it, however, that the lake should be foiled, he struggled on, and when the water shallowed he felt he had come to the end of his strength.
>
> "Another hundred yards would have done for me," he said, and he was so cold that he could not think, and sought his clothes vaguely, sitting down to rest from time to time among the rocks.

"How cold are thy baths, Apollo" is the phrase that returns to mind whenever one thinks of Moore; and in a literature of Anglo-Irish origins, we think of him as one who shook himself free, if only for a brief hour, of the chilling waters of Apollo, and who is now on the unheralded shores of immortality.

A Footnote on
the Historical Novel

> To deal with history means to abandon oneself to chaos and yet to
> retain a belief in the ordination and the meaning. It is a very serious
> task . . . and perhaps also a tragic one.
> —from *Magister Ludi* by Hermann Hesse

IN ENGLISH THE HISTORICAL NOVEL has a fascinating heritage.
Its godfather, if not its actual progenitor, was Sir Walter Scott;
and it is an accepted fact that the *Waverley Novels* rapidly
furthered the spread of the romantic movement. If Sir Walter
lived today, what a marvelous figure he would make in Hollywood! He would still be living beyond his means and twice
as far in debt, being paid in the publicity-ridden, faked gold
dollars that Hollywood generates in millions. His unfinished
estate at Abbotsford—that living dream of anachronic splen-
dor, even in his day—would be twice as large. A brilliant Scots
historian, Donald Carswell, remarked that Sir Walter knew
everything about history—except its meaning. And so he did;
at his worst, he was the literal begetter of the "costume novel"
—which from Sir Walter's day to our own always rises to the
top rungs of the "best sellers" lists.

At his own best Sir Walter was scarcely an historical novelist
at all. His great novels, *The Heart of Midlothian, Guy Man-
nering, Rob Roy, Redgauntlet,* the spectacular "morbid"
romance, *The Bride of Lammermoor,* very nearly existed in

his present tense. They were of an immediate, Scottish, eighteenth-century past, alive in the memories of Sir Walter's elder contemporaries. It was in the word of mouth, legendary aspects of Scottish scenes and incidents that Sir Walter's imagination gained authority. Except for his facile skill in story telling, his famous *Ivanhoe* is bookish claptrap, and the same may be said for many of his other ventures into historical romance, all of which are easily convertible into "costume" narratives. Sir Walter was an avid reader of works in his own genre; nor was he as unsophisticated in his knowledge of human behavior and motives as careless readers of his "costume" narratives may suppose. Proof of his critical insights may be shown in his *Lives of the Novelists* and in his appreciation of M. G. Lewis' *The Monk*—which despite its Spanish setting, is the unique example, and supremely so, of an intensely Gothic novel written on Dutch soil and published in London. Sir Walter did not fail to read it in its suppressed first edition. Yet it is also clear that Sir Walter's "costume" novels were written for the family circle—which *The Monk* was not—and he reserved his more deeply felt revelations of life for scenes that he knew well, the country north of Edinburgh and in the city itself.

With the exceptions of Dickens and Thackeray, the popular historical novelists of the Victorian age followed the models created by Sir Walter's "costume" novels—that line remained unbroken, steering its way under titles that are now forgotten. Only the exceptions—Dickens' *Barnaby Rudge* and *A Tale of Two Cities,* as well as Thackeray's *Henry Esmond,* can be said to contain lives of their own. As historians, both Dickens and Thackeray (and in Dickens' case, half unwillingly) accepted *meanings* of history inspired by Macaulay and Carlyle. These twin distorters of history should not be underestimated in the strength of their influence on the Victorian age; it would have been remarkable (since neither Dickens nor Thackeray were professionals in historical research) if they had completely escaped the dominant, and domineering influences gendered by the two historians. Today, Dickens' *Barnaby Rudge* with its Lord George Gorden riots of 1780, is reread, as it should be, in terms of the Chartists agitations which aroused Dickens' sympathies, yet warned him and his readers against the violence of mob rule; *A Tale of Two Cities* is also reread in the light of social maladjustments in mid-nineteenth-century England—yet its interpretation of the French Revolution stems directly from the teachings of Carlyle. Today Thackeray's *Henry Esmond* is less "historical" in import than psychological, and because it is the most tightly, neatly woven of Thackeray's novels, it holds its place on library shelves. Another exception to the "costume" novel in British historical romances arrived in 1881 in the publication of J. Henry Shorthouse's *John Inglesant*. This romance whose action extends through the years of the English civil war is a "sport" in British fiction, remarkable for its scenes in Italy as well as in England, a theological novel of the first order, disguised as a romance. In fiction, the Anglican Church has no better brief for its position than *John Inglesant*. If not a major novel, it has the distinction of standing alone among nineteenth-century romances.

In the twentieth century the heirs and heiresses of Sir Walter Scott's romances include many "costume" novels of the American Civil War—whether from the North or South, they breed by hundreds. In this genre innovations are few, and whatever period in history they choose to represent, incidents, costumes, legends, myths are overblown, enlarged, so it seems for Hollywood production. It is better to speak of them as "entertainments," panoramas of battles, adventurous love affairs, heroics and histrionics tossed against a huge backdrop called the "past." The most high spirited of these, certainly the most hardy, tough, and yet engaging, is Robert Graves' *I, Claudius*. It has already survived more than a quarter century test of time. But what of more recent contributions to historical fiction that are innovations and not purely "entertainments"?

The best, the most vital of recent innovations in the historical novel are written by Winifred Bryher,[1] one of the few novelists of the present generation who has given pertinent, historical meaning to scenes and incidents of the past. Her four novels, *The Thirteenth of October, The Player's Boy, Roman Wall,* and *Gate to the Sea,* are short, highly charged analogies to situations and problems of loyalty that bedevil our days and nights. She has the insights of a poet, an extraordinary poet, who with fine discrimination selects an illuminating moment of action, and recreates it in a metaphor that may be applied to twentieth-century dilemmas and choices. In her novel, *The Player's Boy,* her story of a changing age may be likened to a change of spirit which fell in darkness over Europe immediately following World War II. For her historical analogy to this mutation she chose the reign of James I in England.

The metamorphosis of James VI of Scotland into James I of England, lord of all Britain and its islands, was the sign of a new age falling, not without disaster, from the old. The histrionic abilities of James outmatched the sunsetting glories of the post-Shakespearean stage; he relished treason plots, and probably inspired several of them. He combined metaphysical wit with courtly love of the young Scots gallants he brought down with him from the north, and if he was, like Nero, an indifferent poet, no one could deny his brilliance on the public stage.

The age was also that of Beaumont and Fletcher, of the years that Sir Walter Raleigh, imprisoned by James, wasted in the Tower, and of the coming of the Puritans, who in a later

---

1 Born Winifred Ellerman at Margate, Kent, in 1894. The name Bryher, taken from one of the Scilly Isles, was first assumed as a pen name, later adopted legally.

decade were to close the theaters. It is in this dramatic setting that the action of Bryher's novel spins its plot.

The story is told in the person of James Sands, a player's boy, apprentice to an actor of the old school and who, for an all too brief spring holiday, is under the protection of the poet, Francis Beaumont. The story is Sands's story, Beaumont's story—and as Bryher writes it, it is the story of every highly sensitized, gifted poet who is the heir of one age and moves into the violence and destructive passions of the age that follows it.

It is impossible to convey the compact artistry of Bryher's prose without quotation:

> The buildings in Cripplegate were unaltered, but otherwise it was a different street. The bright, clear colors of Elizabeth's day were gone with their wearers. Everything was dark and soft, the hated Spanish influence was as apparent here as at Court. These fine, discreet velvets suggested candlelight and conference, the open air of bowling greens would ruin them, these silver laces would tarnish in the rain. . . . Time tangled; it never ran in a straight scythe cut, as they pretended in the moralities, but lay in loops, like the grass at haying time when the conies scampered for safety, and stem and flower were upside down together.

This passage, beautifully tuned to the imagination of James Sands also shows the metaphysical temper of the book as well as its play, one against the other, of pastoral and urban images. No living writer of historical romances can lay claim to the quality of prose that makes *The Player's Boy* a memorable book.

So far I have deliberately withheld a retelling of the book's idyllic love scenes and the tragic implications of its plot—these are for the fortunate reader of the book to rediscover with the assurance that no page lacks dramatic action.

One of the finest scenes in the book is of the crowds that gather to witness Sir Walter Raleigh's execution—and, incidentally, few historical novels I have read have recreated moments of the past with greater accuracy of events and of the men affected by them. The portrait of Francis Beaumont is unmistakably true to the man who joined with Fletcher in writing *The Knight of the Burning Pestle*. The violent ending of the book is appropriate to an age in which James I was the royal actor. James might have had Shakespeare as his court poet, John Donne his chaplain, Lancelot Andrews his intimate advisor in theology, and Bacon his lawyer; his ego dimmed his concern with any of these men. He ignored many of the best writers of his day, and the age fell into violence and darkness.

The violent note on which the novel closes has metaphorical reference to the dark scenes in World War II, scenes of treason and treason trials, and in Europe the aftermath of the German occupation of France. The materialistic Puritans in *The Player's Boy* may be likened to Communists, and the cynical manipulations of James I to insure state rule have their likenesses to bureaucratic state power which threatens the artist in any monolithic state.

Her novel *Gate to the Sea* revives an incident of the fourth century B.C. The scene is the port of Paestum, a town known for the beauty of its rose gardens, a Greek colony on the west shores of the boot of Italy, then recently subjected to the tyranny of new and barbarous invaders, the Lucanians. The central figure of the story is Harmonia, priestess of Hera, goddess of religious song, who has chosen to stay in the conquered city so as to preserve Poseidonian relics and to uphold the elder Greek tradition against ignorance and savagery. The greater majority of her friends had become exiles of Paestum, and Greeks had become slaves of invaders, forbidden to speak their own language, forbidden even to remember their old ways of living, their rites, their customs.

The world of the fourth century B.C. at Paestum was not

unlike invaded worlds today: a change had come—not for a promised better world but for a spiritually dead, starving, and bitter one in which loyalties vanished, friends betrayed friends; all feared to speak their minds.

Bryher's art in the telling of Harmonia's story is one of understatement; no incident of her trials and disillusionments seems theatrical or contrived, yet each has the strength of quietly exerted power, and that power is related to the quality of Bryher's prose: it is clear, taut, free of rhetorical gestures; it is poetic, yet austere—and many miles away from the pitfalls of the "mandarin style." No one living today writes prose with more quiet, unstressed authority than Bryher's. In telling the story of her heroine's decision to change her mind, to escape from Paestum, to carry the Poseidonian relics to a shrine beyond the reaches of barbarian conquerors, Bryher unfolds a dramatic narrative with high moments of action without losing poise or clarity.

Harmonia's resolution at the close of Bryher's story is an example of what her prose accomplishes. Rescued by loyal sailors, and thinking of her escape from Paestum, Harmonia reflects:

> Someday she might understand the purpose of their suffering, sitting perhaps in a garden at Salente with—and how strange it would be—nothing to fear. . . . The past was over; some intuition told her that a recognition of this fact was the purpose of her liberation; she had to persuade the exiles that it was false to dream of a return and that they must root themselves in the new region that had offered them shelter with such willingness. She stared across the bay: there was their beach outlined by a rim of foam. . . . Then as a welcome darkness blotted out the city, she saw in the last flash of light the towers and the white gateway through which they had passed to freedom, old, indestructible, facing the masterless sea.

This is a passage that every twentieth-century exile should learn to understand. No living novelist has expressed their situation better.

In Bryher's work one sees in progress a fresh approach in the creation of historical fiction; fiction that implies the use of an historical imagination as well as the art to give it meaning.

The Character of
F. Scott Fitzgerald

A CURIOUS KIND OF LITERARY fame attends a Scots Presbyterian university in New Jersey. The names associated with it are: Philip Freneau, the first of American poets to write a satire, "The Adventures of Simon Swaugum, a Village Merchant," on the American business man, Edmund Wilson, and F. Scott Fitzgerald. The association of these names has given character to an oasis (which is a strange mixture of nineteenth-century Gothic, and sprucely painted fake American Colonial, but utterly charming) in the flat New Jersey plain. It is, of course, Princeton, and because a Confederate flag is often seen waving from a student dormitory window, it is the most northern of our southern universities. Most of the students have an air of brightly acquired gentility. Princeton's charm is not to be underestimated, nor should one underestimate the charms, with a flash of genius showing through them, of its most notorious undergraduate, a Middle Westerner of Irish heritage, F. Scott Fitzgerald, who gave his heart to Princeton in his first novel, *This Side of Paradise,* and almost lost it there.

As one thinks of certain passages in Fitzgerald's prose, one recalls John McCormack whose tenor voice rivaled James Joyce's when both were young, singing Handel's "Caro Amore" with a Dublin accent; to the purist, something very strange happens to the Italian language and to Handel's song.

149

Yet McCormack's voice as it exists on records is irresistible, and the same kind of lyricism—call it "natural," or "irrational," or what you will, enters passages of Fitzgerald's prose. At the very least, it is a tenor's lyricism that casts its spell; it is light; it is graceful; whether artful or untrained, it is there to be heard.

But what precisely are the other charms that Fitzgerald so undoubtedly possessed? Since all his writings released the facets of a personality, that question is of true importance. First of all, was the charm of his appearance: the blue-green eyes with long eyelashes, the fair hair, the slight figure that was to remain boyish for so many years, the smartness and cleanliness in dress. The other charms sprang from his flashes of romantic egotism, his candor in talking about himself as he believed himself to be, his desire to be richer than any rich boy he had ever met, and to transform that desire into a burlesque of riches. Fitzgerald, born in 1896 in St. Paul, Minn., came of a family that had little enough money to spare: on his father's side there were connections in Maryland and with the family of Francis Scott Key; on his mother's side, with the Irish immigrants of the "famine years" of the early 1850's, who were looked down on in New York and Boston. The Fitzgeralds did not do well in making money, and in F. Scott Fitzgerald's generation in the Middle West, the greatest crime on earth was poverty and the greatest good was the possession of great wealth. He was sent to prep school by an aunt, and later in 1913 to Princeton. Though this shielded Fitzgerald from the fact that his family could not give him countless millions, he was still the "poor boy" at school.

Fitzgerald's situation was peculiarly American Anglo-Irish. There was pride within it, a touch of snobbery that had no rational foundation. Because of his gifts and charms, he might well feel himself superior to other boys at Princeton, yet this was not enough. Within the Anglo-Irish complex an irrational feeling of superiority exists in conflict with a desire to please.

He *had* to charm; he *had* to dress with formal smartness; he *had* to excel. The same complex was shown in Oscar Wilde's social conduct at Oxford. Like Wilde, Fitzgerald was too clear-sighted to sentimentalize his family's Irish origins.

Among the literary origins of Fitzgerald's early novels and short stories, his readings in Ralph Henry Barbour, Booth Tarkington and Rupert Brooke should not be slighted nor quickly tossed aside. Barbour was a good, though now out-moded, writer of boys' books; his stories of life at prep school and at college contained glimpses of the football hero Fitz-gerald wished himself to be. Booth Tarkington was in Fitz-gerald's time a famous Princeton alumnus, a Middle West-erner, and twenty years before Fitzgerald's arrival there, was a most precocious figure on the campus. His example in writ-ing a successful play for the Triangle Club, stirred Fitzgerald's ambitions to the same end—with the result that he neglected his studies. Rupert Brooke's poetry taught Fitzgerald the art of conveying a lyrical, ideally attractive personality into print. His readings in Oscar Wilde, H. G. Wells, Compton Mackenzie were comparatively superficial. Today it is a bit too easy to forget the spell that Barbour and Tarkington cast over and around Fitzgerald: both were expert craftsmen in writing prose that clearly guided rapid narrative; their writings con-veyed the sense of being very much alive, and the prose they wrote was brilliant and light in texture; and both were de-scendants of the school of Robert Louis Stevenson. How com-pletely Fitzgerald emulated Tarkington may be shown in all the stories, the best as well as the worst, that were published in *The Saturday Evening Post* from which an impressive list of his best stories could be made. It would include "Head and Shoulders," "The Offshore Pirate," "The Ice Palace," and "Babylon Revisited."

A year after the publication of *This Side of Paradise* in 1921, "Head and Shoulders" and "The Offshore Pirate" appeared in the pages of the *Post*. Fitzgerald brought to life in fiction

Zelda Sayre (daughter of an Alabama judge, and belle of a World War I "younger set" in a small Southern town) whom he married in 1920. In "Head and Shoulders" Zelda was the pretty show girl, and in "The Offshore Pirate," she was the flapper-heroine, impertinent to her elders, and just nineteen, very pretty to look at, both difficult and easy to lay hands on, and terribly cute to hold; she also gave the impression of knowing her own mind. Before the beginning of the twentieth century Bernard Shaw had invented the same young woman in the person of Mrs. Warren's daughter in *Mrs. Warren's Profession*, the girl with the short hair who became the flapper of World War I, and in England, she was Lady Diana Manners, but it took F. Scott Fitzgerald to make an entire generation of Americans fall in love with her; Zelda was the heroine of the 1920's, and she had both the good fortune and bad luck to be Fitzgerald's wife.

How and why Fitzgerald married her (and the confused round of drinking and domestic hell that followed the marriage) are the elements of the Fitzgerald tragedy. Yet at no time during those years did Fitzgerald's talents utterly desert him. He once remarked that he was a mediocre guardian of his talents, and at another time "talent that matures early is usually of the poetic type which mine was"—and both statements were true. He was careless of the ease with which he could emulate Tarkington so brilliantly, write a lyrical paragraph of prose, and then thinly disguise an episode of autobiography in a short story. He possesed gifts that were distinctly more important than the exercise of talent; they were of an extremely delicate and highly conscious order, gifts that were frail, precise and very like the mechanism of a small, platinum-cased watch, and which, like a watch, measured the waste of his own life. The gifts included self-knowledge and the importance of converting that knowledge into a work of art—and they produced *The Great Gatsby, The Crack-up* letters to his friends and daughter, and six memorable chapters of an unfinished novel, *The Last Tycoon.*

Of Fitzgerald's friends at Princeton, Edmund Wilson alone had a steady enough eye to perceive the value of Fitzgerald's gifts—and through Fitzgerald's life, Wilson was his "literary conscience." Beyond the gossip and distractions of the jazz age, Fitzgerald's gifts laid bare an understanding of the vanity of human wishes, which included the desires to be forever young, to be fabulously rich, to be continually in love—and in Fitzgerald's case, it was as though a Princeton boy had unearthed a fragment of the Faust legend and translated it into the language of the twentieth century. From the time of writing *The Beautiful and Damned* in 1921 to the writing of *The Crack-up* through 1936 and 1937, the fear of failure enters much of what Fitzgerald had to say: "I speak with the authority of failure," he once said, but in the light of his accomplishment, only the literal-minded would accept the verdict of "failure" as a description of his life and work.

One of the errors in Fitzgerald's life was in his marriage, which was as though Lord Byron had made the mistake of marrying the Byronic heroine, Caroline Lamb, who was more than willing to recast her personality, her life in Byron's image. But Fitzgerald, dazzled by the celebrity he achieved with his first novel, *This Side of Paradise,* and the sudden transient riches gained from the sale of his short stories, was by no means as worldly as the British poet who had preceded him by more than a hundred years. He walked directly into an extremely subtle trap that was attractively furnished on all four of its walls by the glittering convex mirrors of twentieth-century narcissism. First the Fitzgeralds drank to put themselves at ease among wealthier company than they had known before Fitzgerald went to Princeton, company which soon became an ironic reward of literary and social success; this was the period in which the Fitzgeralds traveled through every fashionable resort in Europe and America. Almost imperceptibly a second cause for drinking and wild parties slowly arrived, a cause that was as complex as the fear of failure and involved the nightmares of two personalities that had become one. Impulses toward insanity and self-destruction began to fester beneath the surface of their lives.

Had Fitzgerald been less conscious, less possessed by a sense of guilt as well as a sense of responsibility to his wife and later to his daughter, there would be a far less romantic story for his critics to remember. As early as 1922, ominous signs of Zelda's insanity appeared in Westport, Conn., where the Fitzgeralds were temporarily at home. Zelda put in a fire alarm and when the firemen arrived and asked her where the fire was, she struck her breast and said, "Here." Eight years after Fitzgerald's death in 1948 she died in a fire that destroyed the asylum where she was kept. The early warning, as well disguised as the voice of an oracle, had all the external appearance of a childish and drunken joke.

Meanwhile, through the 1920's Fitzgerald fell in debt to his literary agent, Harold Ober, who, next to Edmund Wilson, was the most thoughtful of Fitzgerald's friends. Harold Ober advanced far more than necessary money to Fitzgerald; he gave him understanding and recognition. The 1920's had slipped away beneath the feet of the traveling Fitzgeralds; and in spite of the success of *The Great Gatsby* (which brought Fitzgerald critical respect and praise), the 1930's brought a gray after-holiday Monday morning to them. Zelda's lack of success in writing, painting and in her attempts to become a professional dancer, drove her over the borderline of a breakdown into insanity. The critics of the 1930's had little sympathy with the heroes and heroines whom Fitzgerald had created in his own image. The critics of that decade had no use at all for the virtues of being young, beautiful, and rich. They had unearthed the virtues of "social responsibility," and their manner of doing so was very like the virtue of Mme. de Genlis as it was described by Napoleon: "When Mme. de Genlis wishes to define virtue she speaks of it as a discovery."

But Fitzgerald was not deceived by the critics who had discovered virtue in fanatical leanings toward Communism; in 1940, the year of his death, he wrote to his daughter:

> I think it was you who misunderstood my meaning about the comrades. It is not that you should not disagree with them—the important thing is that you should not argue with them. The point is that Communism has become an intensely dogmatic and almost mystical religion, and whatever you say, they have ways of twisting it into shapes which put you in some lower category of mankind ("Fascist, Liberal Trotskyist"), and disparage you both intellectually and personally in the process. They are amazingly well organized.

Anyone who has lived through the 1930's and the early 1940's in this country knows the wisdom of Fitzgerald's observations. Because of his domestic responsibilities (so admirably told in his short story, "Babylon Revisited") he turned to writing scripts in Hollywood so that he could earn enough money to pay for Zelda's care in an asylum and his daughter's education at boarding school and college.

Outside of those who knew him in Hollywood, Fitzgerald's reputation had acquired the aura of "snob appeal." To young instructors of English in boys' prep schools and colleges, Fitzgerald's heroes represented all the attractions of the lives their students were to lead. In this perspective, the Fitzgerald visions of wealth became hugely magnified. The young instructors consoled themselves for the lives denied them by praising Fitzgerald's talents for burlesque and irony.

Today it is easy to see a consistent vein in Fitzgerald's complex character that perceived the deceptive glories of success at Princeton as well as his own "crack-up" in Hollywood. At whatever costs to him, it is our advantage that the later Fitzgerald who wrote *The Great Gatsby,* "Babylon Revisited," fragments of *The Last Tycoon,* was an immeasurably better writer than the author of *This Side of Paradise*. At the very least the later Fitzgerald was not self-deceived. Behind him in his Irish heritage of pride and middle-class "lace-curtain" respectability—and this with the teachings of the American Irish Catholic Church—were the foundations of his conscience, his responsibilities. His acute self-knowledge could not repair (except in his best writings) the damage caused by his impulse to live at "top speed," to be the self-destructive hero of his *Zeitgeist*. It is now likely that his writings will survive the nostalgia that the present moment has for the reckless living of the 1920's. If one searches for analogies in literature to describe the light, firm brilliance to be found in the best of Fitzgerald's lyrical prose, one turns to *A Sportsman's Notebook*, the early writings of Turgenev. The same heightened, poetic consciousness of life and its betrayals is evident in both.

A Portrait of the Irish
as
James Joyce

WHAT OF THE IRISH? THE first association is that of sentimental rubbish: pigs and poverty, green harps, broken clay
pipes, priests, bogs, pale-colored whiskey, sorrowing mothers,
white-skinned half-naked girls, dirt, tears, murder, and maudlin songs. After that, a pious, betraying, shrewd, Godhaunted,
Devil-possessed, God-cursed, embittered, timid, brave, lech-
erous, prudish, naive, innocent, guilt-ridden, proud people—
which is a fraction nearer a romantic truth. And added to this
was an old idea: "Every Irishman is a King; every Irishman is
a poet"—particularly the latter. Evidence of Kingship vanished
centuries ago, but the halo of Kingship remained. Scarcely
more tangible was the conviction, "Every Irishman, a poet":

> Ich am of Irlonde
> Ant of the holy londe
>   Of Irlonde.
> Gode sire, pray ich the,
> For of saynte charite,
> Come ant dance wyth me
> In Irlonde.

This was a fragment of a beggar girl's song—set down by
God knows whom. It whined a bit, yet it was poetry and held

real music in it. How does it stand with the claim that every Irishman is a poet? Not very strongly. Behind it however was a fanatical belief; poetry and Ireland were one. Past the middle of the seventeenth century, a great half-poet, Jonathan Swift was born in Dublin. Near the middle of the eighteenth century Oliver Goldsmith, outwardly a brave-timid, naive-witty Irishman who talked foolishly, and whenever he had money, tossed it away, wrote "The Deserted Village," a poem that steadily improves with time. It looked as though the Irish claim were lost. One poet only was the score: and one supremely modest poem. Of course there were poems in Gaelic—but could these make a literature? They were too fragmentary. The fanatical belief persisted, a belief that was the triumph of wild imagination over possibilities: then came Yeats, the excitement of the Celtic Renaissance, and a crowd of minor writers (seemingly descended from Tom Moore), then Bernard Shaw and George Moore (who today is rated lower than he should be) and James Joyce. To the bewilderment of the Irish themselves, the Irish claims came true, and a truth that is extended in the writings of Samuel Beckett. A tradition of belief suddenly paid off: it was like watching a river of quarters and half-dollars pour from the opened doors of a two cent slot-machine.

The score may now be counted: five writers of the first order: Yeats, Shaw, Joyce, O'Faolain (the short story), Beckett. And these claims are not in terms of money made or of "the Bitch-Goddess Success." They are to be measured in terms of vision, humane compassion (no matter how "coldly Irish" it may seem), and strength of character—and ultimately, beyond the provinces of art. Both Yeats and Joyce rested their early claims for superiority not on the skills of their art, but on having mastered them, stressed their claims upon a "showing-forth" of life itself, that is why a study of their lives has its importance toward an understanding of what they wrote.

Although Richard Ellmann's *James Joyce* is probably not the last book he will write, it has the air of being "a masterpiece." In the best sense of the word it is an "official" biography, a large book that reconstructs, year by year, Joyce's life from his birth in Rathmines, near Dublin, February 2, 1882 to his death in the Schwesterhaus, Zurich, January 12, 1941. Inspiration of high talent enters Ellmann's book; it is a living tribute to Joyce's memory, and one of few excellent books of its kind in literary history.

Whether Ellmann intended to make James Joyce an archetypical Irishman or not, his book succeeds in making Joyce combine within himself all the contradictory elements in Irish character: his pride playing against his guilt-ridden soul, his blasphemy against Thomism and Jesuit-trained piety, his almost boundless courage against fear of thunderstorms and dogs, his arrogance in the face of good fortune and bad, against timidity and shyness with women, his heavy drinking against an ascetic passion for the "hard way" and hard work, his brutality (for his treatment of his brother Stanislaus was no less than brutal) against the extremes of tenderness for other members of his family, his intellectual integrity against a naive clinging to superstitions, his ease in weeping against the power to evoke a comic genius greater than the wits of Sheridan, Goldsmith, Wilde and Shaw, his poverty against an aristocratic flinging away of money, a love of maudlin Irish songs against a brilliant critical taste in the writing of parodies, his dandyism (for the male Irish even in rags always look "smart") against the wearing of white, easily soiled tennis shoes, his love of perfection and neoclassical pedantry against the widest flights of imagination in romantic literature. Joyce, as Richard Ellmann so convincingly presents him is the Irish hero—*gloria in excelsis!*

To say that Joyce was a complex human being is an understatement, and it was a sign of his genius and strength of character that he kept his complexities intact. When Joyce in desperation over the incurable madness of his daughter Lucia forced himself to consult Dr. C. G. Jung, he succeeded in confusing that eminent psychiatrist—but of course, few Irish heroes have spent an afternoon reclining on a psychiatrist's couch. They match their wits, their sins, their guilt against the mouth of a confession box with an Irish priest on the other side of it. It is unlikely that any psychiatrist, however famous, will ever come to know a Joycean Irish hero: the moment he *thinks* he does so, he slips into a trap that even the most ignorant, simple-minded Irish priest would cheerfully avoid. Though the mature Joyce kept away from the confession box himself, and properly called himself a Jesuit, not a Catholic, he advised troubled friends to confess to priests—and not to waste their time and money in psychiatrists' offices.

Joyce matched his strength against two highly gifted members of his own family—his prodigal drunken father who reduced his family to living in a Dublin slum, and Stanislaus Joyce, his younger brother, who became a violently bigoted atheist, and the very soul of human virtues. Joyce outcharmed both. Outwardly, Stanislaus was the "strong man," regular in habits, just and coolheaded, kind and loyal; and as his own book, *My Brother's Keeper,* proves, very nearly a writer of the first order. Actually he was the weaker of his father's sons, giving his earnings away to support his sisters, James and James's family; it is significant that his book, his single gift to posterity, even at his death in 1955, remained an unfinished manuscript. James's strength of character from childhood through middle age was masked by youthful arrogance and the charm of one who laughed away the fears of those around him. His own fears (at their darkest) were purged by occasional bouts of heavy drinking. Since he possessed, like his father, a fine voice and a nearly flawless "ear," a few hours of drinking were topped by a round of songs. Spurred by his father, and trained in Jesuit schools where his father's eloquence secured scholarships for him, Joyce's intellectual disciplines were furthered. Deeply inspired family pride played its part here, as well as intellectual boldness and arrogance. Joyce could not, did not fail the father who wrote an indignant letter to the Pope, protesting against the desertion of Roman Catholic Ireland from Parnell's cause. To logical, sane, uninspired eyes, old John Joyce's railings at the Pope seems wilfull comic madness, but with full knowledge of Ireland's distress, the sacred person of an Italian Pope meant nothing to an Irish Joyce. James Joyce inherited the strength of his father's wit and arrogance—in the same breath he was "in" the Irish Catholic Church and "out" of it, as individual as Adam, the first created man, and intellectually a Thomist, a follower of Dante and Giambattista Vico and a Jesuit. Joyce was a whole-souled blasphemer (as the Irish so often are), and *not* like his younger brother, an earnest, honest, atheist heretic.

While still an undergraduate at University College, Dublin, Joyce wrote an appreciation of Ibsen which had the good fortune to find publication in *The Fortnightly Review* of London—a tremendous tour de force for a boy of eighteen. In Dublin the essay established him as a genius. More remarkable than the essay itself were the inspiration and the will that arose from it, Joyce's learning of Dano-Norwegian so he could read Ibsen in the original, and then write a letter to Ibsen.

This last action showed that his reputation of being a "genius" in Dublin did not deceive him, that his intentions had seriousness behind them, that he was not to spare himself the rigors of the "hard way," that he would force himself to "make good" the claims of his pride and egotism. His patronizing friend, Oliver Gogarty, was no fool. He felt, rather than perceived, Joyce's hidden strength; he soon learned that he had blundered in offending Joyce's sensibilities, and for that reason feared him. In his insensitive clumsy way, he became obsequious to Joyce. Did he know he would go down to posterity as "stately, plump Buck Mulligan"—the anti-Joyce, the eternal Judas? Of course not. But he felt that something terrible might happen.

W. B. Yeats's handling of Joyce's arrogance showed far deeper insight than Gogarty's. The inner Yeats was as tough as the inner Joyce; Yeats knew the ways of Irish charm and what they concealed, and it is not surprising that the elder poet was the sharpest critic of Joyce's early poems; he did not underrate their sensitivity, their subtle musical innovations, their distinction—his only complaint was that they did not *say* enough. Patiently, and in the face of Joyce's impertinence, he became Joyce's most steadfast champion, passing his writings on to be praised by a young American of his generation, Ezra Pound.

Joyce's various places of exile away from Dublin—Paris, Trieste, Rome, periodic brief stays in London, Zurich—never left Ireland behind, but rather intensified the *presence* of Dublin wherever Joyce lived in wildly extravagant Irish poverty. This was a kind of poverty that always went in debt five pounds after the last penny was spent. The presence was heightened by his heroic "common-law" wife, Nora Barnacle, who was as archetypically Irish as he—his Eve, his mistress wife-mother, his Molly Bloom, and essentially, his Anna Livia Plurabelle, mother of his son Giorgio and his Cassandra-fated daughter, Lucia. These, with Stanislaus (who followed them and so often supported them out of his poor earnings from the language-teaching, piece-work factory of the Berlitz School where both brothers were employed) were his true intimates. He could not exist without them, nor they without him. He was their prodigal patriarch. After Joyce's death, Nora found the routine of living dull; she had not read his books, but shared the excitement of a precarious "good life," with self-sacrificing patronesses such as Harriet Weaver and Sylvia Beach, the publisher of *Ulysses,* rescuing her "Jim" from ruin. When asked if she remembered visits from André Gide, she looked blank, and then replied, "Sure, if you've been married to the greatest writer in the world you don't remember all the little fellows."

Rather too much than too little has been written of Joyce as the supreme artist of his day. After his death, "the Revolution of the Word" collapsed in fragments of some of the worst writing the world has ever read. The only writer to "come out" of

Joyce, and to go his own way, the "hard way," is Samuel Beckett. Joyce left no heirs. His two masterpieces, *Ulysses* and *Finnegans Wake*, are resurrections of the Comic Spirit of which we have such rare examples as the writings of Rabelais, *Don Quixote, Tristram Shandy,* and *Gulliver's Travels.* That compassionate spirit is humane, not humanitarian. As Joseph Campbell suggests, *Finnegans Wake* achieves its universality by being the misadventures of the soul in Purgatory. Yet *Finnegans Wake's* achievement is precarious. The accent of the book is parochial, and its primary demand upon the reader is to hear it read aloud; its very accent is "of Ireland." If one cares nothing for the Irish and its "monster"-composite-hero, Finnegan-HCE, and is slow to recognize the dazzling beauty of Anna Livia Plurabelle, the true measure of its great achievement is half lost. Even today its danger lies in becoming the unread classic of the twentieth century; it needs an exposition as brilliant as the outline found in the Campbell-Robinson *A Skeleton Key to Finnegans Wake.*

Ellmann's contribution to Joyceana is one that shows the distinctly personal sources of Joyce's writings—a revelation that makes Joyce as "personal" a writer as W. B. Yeats. His missteps are few, and these are related to his tone-deaf readings of Joyce's lyricism. In this respect, Ellmann belongs to the tone-deaf generation of critics who came forward in the 1940's, who accepted the flaws of Pound, Eliot, and Auden as standards of excellence in writing verse and grew to admire flat lines and tone-deaf phrasing. Joyce's gift was nine-tenths auditory—so was his wit. His slight lyrics, underrated by Ellmann, have greater distinction than the best of A. E. Housman.

Since the arrivals of *Ulysses* and *Finnegans Wake* much has happened that has dimmed the shock of the first impact of Joyce's genius. Members of the Joyce Cult are growing old. Today Joyce's prestige is academic. What remains? Experiment for art's sake is dead. One must look further. Joyce as the great forerunner in twentieth-century literature reveals another aspect. His writings are still God-haunted; he is the fore-runner of a renewed theological approach to life. In this lies the secret of his endurance. His art was the means, the embodiment of his secret, the heart of his example in reading Dante's *Divine Comedy*. *Ulysses* and *Finnegans Wake* are works of the yea-sayer. One must be tone-deaf indeed not to hear the notes of an Irish resurrection of mankind in *Finnegans Wake*.

The Dying Gladiators
of
Samuel Beckett

1

THE FIRST THING TO BE said about Samuel Beckett—and I suspect it will be the last—is that he is essentially a poet. This statement may seem illogical because the general public knows him as the author of a play, *Waiting for Godot,* written in prose, and is beginning to know him as the author of a trilogy, *Molloy* (1955), *Malone Dies* (1956), and *The Unnamable* (1958). In Beckett's case, unlike that of many others who begin a literary career by writing a slender book of poems (Beckett's was *Whoroscope,* 1930), the fact retains its importance in his later prose. It is reinforced by a second volume of verse, *Echo's Bones,* which was published in Paris by George Reavey under the imprint of the Europa Press (1935).

Beckett's prose comes from the same imaginative fount that his early poems do; the later prose is far better than the poems, but it is prose written as poems are written, conveying emotion directly to the reader. His stories and his play have the structure of poems rather than strictly narrative and dramatic forms. That is one reason out of many why audiences were first disquieted then moved by *Waiting for Godot:* they came to see a play; what they heard was something that did not imitate poetry as they knew it, but was the economical, sometimes ambiguous language of a poetic imagination.

The second thing to be said is that Beckett is a comic writer of the first order, one who has intense poetic understanding and revelation of human destiny. At the highest moments of Beckett's farcical situations, he is most serious, most revealing and in a certain sense (of which there is more to say) *religious* in his view of the human comedy. In his writings, the emotions caused by terror, pity, despair, the death-wish, and love are purged by laughter. Beckett achieves a nearly classical distinction, ancient enough, but he has renewed it in twentieth-century terms, of what comedy should be; his heroes are mock-tragic heroes, "Dying Gladiators," yet never attaining respect among living creatures around them, or a desired funereal dignity. They are never completely damned or blessed. They inhabit purgatory.

In speaking of Beckett's "Dying Gladiators" I use the phrase advisedly. A gladiator's martyrdom was not that of a kinglike tragic hero. The tragic fall was not his; death was for the amusement of those who witnessed his fall in a Roman circus. However skillful, however brave he might be, whatever immortality he achieved was an anonymous one. The Gladiator was outside the orbit of Roman society, or rather he was in it only on the level of being an entertainer. The Christians saw his death as an incident in the martyrdom of man. Beckett's heroes also exist, or try to, outside the conventions of a society as complex as any in the ancient world.

But how did Beckett find such creatures, one might ask. In himself? Of course. Yet the question demands a far more objective answer. Beckett's emotional and intellectual heritage is in evidence here; it includes the peculiarities of Protestant Anglo-Irish, south Irish parentage, education at Dublin's Trinity College, Beckett's interest in the German philosophers, his short term as James Joyce's secretary, his probable reading of Bergson's essay on laughter. Beckett's early surroundings, clearly shown in his first book of stories, *More Pricks Than Kicks* (1934), are of the Protestant in a Roman Catholic country, a place that is "out of the world" in one sense, and deeply heretical in another; it is a condition of exile at home. Even when the Anglo-Irishman leaves Ireland his tendency is to become more Irish than the actual Irish, to be haunted by a few drops of Irish blood in his veins. It is characteristic of him to turn to Europe, not England, as his intellectual home.

The Catholic Church in Ireland has always taken pride in being more Catholic than the Pope at Rome; its effect on the Protestant living in south Ireland is to infuse, if only by osmosis, a daily conviction of living, either well, or more frequently poorly, within the orbit of a Christian world. The Protestant position in Ireland is one fork of a three-pronged theological agony, of which the other two are the established order of the Church at Rome and the provincial bigotry of the Irish Catholic. In Ireland the most extreme Calvinist cannot equal the passionate bigotry of the Irish Catholic; in Ireland the most sincere atheist finds his position belittled by the sneaking conviction that he is committing blasphemy by existing at all; even he cannot escape an unheroic damnation. When Yeats wrote . . . "Because this country has a pious mind . . ." he thought of Ireland and not less of Colonus; it was also a country in which "a man can be so crossed; / Can be so battered, badgered and destroyed / That he's a loveless man . . ." and though Yeats was constantly forced into an heretical position, he was also forced into an admiration for Von Hügel. A gifted Protestant in south Ireland always feels the prodding of the triple-pronged fork. Even if he leaves Ireland as Beckett did (he lives in Paris and has written four novels and two plays in French), the conflicts of theological doubt and faith pursue him. His ragged soul still walks in purgatory.

In his prose Beckett has sustained the ancient, sometimes

parallel, association of religion with poetry; and if at times they seem to vanish, they are just around the corner. Scratch an Irish poet, and if the scratch is deep enough to draw blood, the result, however heretical it may be, will be a religious poem.

From the publication dates of Beckett's books we know that the earliest of them appeared when critical attention had been turned to writing of "social content." This partly explains why *More Pricks Than Kicks,* and *Murphy,* both published in London, were ignored. The effort to read immediate "social-consciousness" into Beckett's writings is a waste of time; Beckett's concerns are with the conflicts of flesh and spirit, of mind and soul; one has to strain to read superficial political meanings into them. Other reasons why the books were ignored are also clear. *More Pricks Than Kicks* is a collection of stories, all Irish, which, put together, almost make a novel; they are uneven, and to their credit today, non-professional, their brilliance untarnished, the work of a "divine amateur." Among the stories, "Dante and the Lobster" and "Love and Lethe" await rediscovery; reread today they both absorb and transcend the Irish city and landscapes around them. At the time of their first publication the young Beckett could be dismissed as a charming writer whose direction was unknown; today we recognize in "Love and Lethe" a better version of Graham Greene's short story, "A Drive in the Country."

It makes little difference which story was written first (I suspect Beckett's was); the point is that if one is writing about a dangerous young man who takes a girl for a drive in the country with the intention (unknown to her) of forcing her into a suicide pact, it is better to give it a comic turn as Beckett does than to make it vulgar by converting it into a slick magazine story melodrama. In Greene's story, the girl escapes the clutches of the young man and leaves him to put a bullet through his silly self-destructive head, then returns home, virtue triumphant, her lesson learned, to her dear dull parents. It is very like a Hollywood script and unconvincing. In

Beckett's story the girl forces Irish whiskey down the young man's throat (drinking half the bottle herself) until he is too drunk to aim a gun at anything, and then instructs him in the pleasures of making love. There is a comic ring of truth in Beckett's story. The mock-hero who is the central figure in all the stories of *More Pricks Than Kicks,* and it is he who gives the book an air of being the first draft of a novel, is also the first of Beckett's "Dying Gladiators."

2

". . . and they drew all manner of things—everything that begins with an M—"

"Why with an M?" said Alice.

"Why not?" said the March Hare.

Alice was silent.

The Dormouse had closed its eyes by this time, and was going off into a doze; but, on being pinched by the Hatter, it woke up again with a little shriek, and went on: "—that begins with an M, such as mouse-traps, and the moon, and memory, and madness . . ."

—Lewis Carroll: *Alice in Wonderland*

After *More Pricks Than Kicks* Beckett's settings leave provincial Ireland unnamed; *Murphy* is a stop-off in London, South Kensington—and memorably, Kensington Gardens, a place made famous by two visitors before Beckett, J. M. Barrie and Henry James. I am aware that many readers of Beckett's writings will think first of Joyce, then Kafka; they are not wrong in doing so; Beckett has obvious debts to both, but the point is that he has taken his own direction, and on that way he is playing another tune than theirs. The direct influence of Joyce (great master that he is and will remain) has probably sterilized more young writers than reinspired them; of those who felt his dominance only a few, and Beckett is one, have had enough strength of character, and enough to say in their own right, to survive. The Beckett who holds attention is the

Beckett who has absorbed the teachings of a master and has walked in a road of his own making. A primary reason why Beckett's later writings strike beneath the surface of entertainment is, of course, the emotional charge of their religious associations. Another reason, scarcely less important, is that Beckett's comedy has behind it certain truths of philosophic origin. Those who complain that Beckett is so "negative" in his views, should remember Nietzsche's "yeas" and "nays"— and finally that two negatives can produce an affirmative. In Beckett's *Molloy* and *Malone Dies* there are several excellent parodies on the subject of education; to the reader of German philosophy these seem to stem from Schopenhauer's remarks on education in his essay *The Art of Literature*. I quote from Schopenhauer on men of learning, a passage which may be read as a comment on Beckett's wit in his parodies on education. Murphy refuses to read books; Moran attempts to instruct his son; these scenes seem to have behind them touches of the same quality of wit that is in the following:

> The wig is the appropriate symbol of the man of learning, pure and simple. It adorns the head with a copious quantity of false hair, in lack of one's own: just as erudition means endowing it with a great mass of alien thought. This, to be sure, does not clothe the head so well and naturally, nor is it so generally useful, nor so suited for all purposes, nor so firmly rooted; nor when alien thought is used up can it be immediately replaced by more from the same source, as is the case with that which springs from soil of one's own. Se we find Sterne, in his *Tristram Shandy,* boldly asserting *an ounce of a man's own wit is worth a ton of other people's.*

Beckett's wit is supremely his own; if at times his technic resembles Joyce's, and in some very few cases Kafka's, his application of it is in terms of his own imagination. Consciously or not, though I suspect consciously, for Beckett's heroes carry within them a conflict between mind and body, Beckett sounds the depths of a truth concerning education; to say the least, the farcical situation he presents has intellectual tension behind it, and because Beckett is a poet, the intellectual paradox is stated in terms that evoke the emotional response of laughter.

In the same way, one of the roots of Beckett's comedy may be discovered in Bergson's essay, *Laughter,* which is a reason why Beckett's farcical situations are in impeccable taste and never descend to mere vulgarities. All the flaws in the Broadway production of *Waiting for Godot* may be traced to "slickness" of presentation, which allows for "nice-nellying" a statement, and therefore vulgarizes it. The original depth is covered over, if not lost. Small and vulgar clichés creep in, such as Bert Lahr's famous "Billy Watson's sliding-act" repeated at least once too often. Beckett's detailed parodies of clothing, his descriptions of what his heroes wear, are related, if anywhere, to Bergson's remarks in *Laughter* on dress:

> This vision of the mechanical and the living superimposed one upon the other leads us to consider a yet vaguer image, that of some sort of rigidity clamped to the mobility of life, trying ungracefully to follow life's lines and to imitate its fluidity. One can then see how easy it is for an article of clothing to become ridiculous. One can almost say that any fashion of dress has its laughable side. Only, when it is a question of current modes we are so used to the garments that we tend to accept them as an integral part of the body that they adorn. Our imagination fails to separate the two. The idea no longer occurs to us to oppose the inert rigidity of the envelope to the supple activity of the object enveloped. Here the comic element rests in a latent state. It will immediately break out when the natural incompatibility between the envelope and the enveloped will be so striking that even the traditional reconcilement will not succeed in consolidating their union: such is the case of the top hat, for example. Imagine the case of an eccentric who walks the streets in fashions of bygone days; our attention is then called to the clothing, we distinguish it completely from the wearer, we say that the wearer is *disguising* himself (as if every form of dress was not a disguise), and the laughable side of the fashion passes from the shade into the sunlight.

Beckett also follows certain Bergsonian laws for the logic of imagination as opposed to those of the conscious mind, that is, of organized, mechanical, and "conforming" society. Beckett strikes beneath "the logic of mind" to "a dream dreamed by the whole of society," which is why Beckett has never had the least concern for immediate political and social movements. As artist he is at an opposite extreme from those who have yielded to the fantasies of social science. Again, Bergson is relevant.

> A proposition like this one: "my everyday clothing forms a part of my body" is absurd in the eyes of reason. Nevertheless the imagination holds it as a truth. "A red nose is a painted nose," "a Negro is a white man in disguise," yet more absurdities for the reason, but elemental truths for the simple imagination. There is thus a logic for the imagination which is not the logic of the mind, which sometimes opposes it. . . . It is something like the logic of the dream, but of a dream that will not let itself be abandoned to the caprice of individual fantasy, since it is a dream dreamed by the whole society. . . . It obeys certain laws, or rather, certain customs, which are to the imagination that which logic is to the mind.

From these associations we may turn to the sleepy Dormouse's remarks on M; the Dormouse has fallen into a dream within a dream (since Alice's *Wonderland* is itself a dream) and speaks from it. The conversation took place at a "mad tea-party" which exists within the logic of imagination. The institution-sanitarium scenes in *Murphy* and *Malone Dies* are at the same dream-within-dream levels. Murphy yields to the social need of taking a job, which may be equated with entering an institution—the institution is a mental hospital, and Murphy, as a male nurse, the lowest, most nearly radical position in it, encounters the castrating results of holding a job at all. He is also being prepared for death by fire, a pagan death, a loss of Christian identity. In *Malone Dies* the institution scenes blend from a dingy rooming house to dream-within-dream settings of a mental hospital-*cum*-monastery—and "why not" as the March Hare would say, why should not Beckett's "Dying Gladiators'" names begin with an M? They find themselves in places that are like ill-lighted interiors of old-fashioned cheesecake-shaped mousetraps, lunacy from the moon invades their quarters, they are much concerned with memory and philosophic muchness—they have come a long way from provincial Ireland, and yet certain dimmed, hilly, raining, half-pastoral melancholy images persist. *Alice in Wonderland* may not be Beckett's source for his use of M; but his use of it is as valid as the Dormouse's defense of drawing things from a well; and the most important thing drawn from a well has been truth.

Beckett's writings are centrifugal, not linear in movement; they are coneshaped, very like the spiral described in Yeats's *A Vision,* and the last scenes in *Murphy* and *Malone Dies,* though they seem to be dislocated from what has gone before, are visionary "summings-up," the moments of a "showing-forth" that Joyce wrote of in *Stephen Hero.* The flying kite scene over Kensington Gardens in *Murphy* is one of the finest passages in twentieth-century prose. The choice of a garden for the scene has a classical precedent in French literature which extends from *The Princess of Cleves* to *Strait Is the Gate.* Beckett has done many things at once with that scene; he has "summed-up" Murphy's impotence, since he is now heroically dead by pagan fire, by having his mistress, a mock-widow, nurse an impotent old man flying a kite from his wheelchair. Yet the kite for him is a nearest approach to heaven, the nearest approach to control of a visible universe. Kensington Gardens and the large sky above them may also represent nature surrounded by the most impressive of man-made things, the largest of modern cities. A half-ironic balance is struck to close an hilarious, lightly written comic novel.

In respect to the texture of their prose *Molloy* and *Malone Dies* are far more closely woven than Beckett's earlier writings; certain scenes are reworked, reinforced and given accumulative meaning. A scene in the rain is reset from "A Wet Night"—one of the less successful stories in *More Pricks Than Kicks*—in a memorable passage in *Malone Dies,* and the parodies on education through the early stories are renewed, intensified, and given in greater variation in *Murphy, Molloy,* and *Malone Dies.* Though in purgatory, Beckett's heroes move toward a state of becoming; the passion, the agony of purgatory is theirs, they must still wait for the Epiphany, "the showing-forth," something beyond their trials, their errors, which cannot be named.

Malone Dies is filled with references to the Gospel of St. John, negatively said because Malone, always in a state of becoming, never achieves a place in the true light, "the true light, which lighteth every man that cometh into the world." The Epiphany at the end of *Malone Dies* is a casting off into the gray light of the sea, and the scene recalls "Except a man be born again, he cannot see the Kingdom of God. Nicodemus saith unto him, How can a man be born when he is old? Can he enter a second time into his mother's womb, and be born? Jesus answered, Amen, Amen, I say unto thee, Except a man be born of water and the Holy Spirit, he cannot enter into the Kingdom of God." Malone has not stepped beyond purgatory for the rebirth of his spirit, but has reached water. This passage from the Gospel of St. John also gives pertinent meaning to the first page of *Molloy:* "I am in my mother's room [the effort to enter a second time into his mother's womb]. It's I who live there now. I don't know how I got there."

The crutches, the sticks, the hats, the shoes are erroneous, ridiculous, unnatural projections of the body as Beckett's characters wear them; one guide to their origins may be found in Diderot's speculations on a blindfolded man's use of two sticks for eyes. Malone, since he lives or dies in semidarkness, is half-blind; it is his stick that makes him sure of possessing things on earth. Molloy is dependent upon his crutches and a bicycle; that error frustrates the nature of the body; the inanimate projections deform growth. If Diderot's blindfolded man represents the life of reason, then that life in semidarkness becomes deformed, is a kind of death. So much for the substrata of Beckett's mock-tragic and wholly farcical situations; the point is that they stir emotions which lie beneath them. The last turn that Beckett makes concerns memory.

Beckett's mock-heroes have defective memories—which is a deeply human, often ridiculous limitation of the mind. In *Waiting for Godot*, Gogo insists "I either forget things immediately, or I remember them forever." Truly enough, he forgets what happened yesterday or the day before, or the day before that. His memory, defective, fractional, has hold only on the fact that he *is* waiting; he remembers a continuity of waiting and becoming, a nearly instinctive process, something like (but in him translated into human terms) the abstract life force, constantly becoming that which Bergson described in his *Creative Evolution*. What he is waiting for is called "Godot"; but Gogo can make an error, if only for a moment, that Pozzo (another character in the play) is "Godot." Godot remains ambiguous and not of this earth: he is left open for the reader or audience to fill in his name. Gogo's one positive gesture out of the "nays" that surround him is the strength to wait. Gogo and Vladimir may be regarded as two human negatives, two errors that together, as they touch hands, create the "yes." They reject suicide; the power to wait preserves them. The other pair of friends, Pozzo and Lucky, destroy each other; they may read as destructive elements of friendship on earth, the master-slave complex of violent feeling; they ride on the stage and off; they lack the unworldly strength to wait.

No paraphrases of Beckett's writings can hope to equal the actual performance of what he says. The best one can do is realize that his prose, like poetry, has its own shades of meaning and association. Today, and at a moment when most writers have become willing to conform to whatever demands society makes upon them, Beckett stands almost alone. He too is becoming, and I strongly suspect that although he is as invisible as Godot (except in Paris) he has come to stay.